"Lucien Miller, a married Catholic deacon and professor of Chinese studies, documents his experience of the person and teachings of Shigeto Vincent Oshida, a Japanese Zen teacher and Catholic priest. Miller translates in poignant detail the life and work of this no longer hidden spiritual master. *Jesus in the Hands of Buddha* presents boundary-crossing insights and practices at the core of cross-cultural spiritual living. He profoundly offers an experience of accessible guidance and consolation for world readers of all faiths living on the ropes."

> — Jonathan Montaldo, author of *Bridges to Contemplative Living with Thomas Merton*

"Oshida's life and legacy is an experience of the spiritual senses knowing the mystical voice. Biblical in sources and Buddhist in form, reading this book took me as a reader to the great pause of silence."

> — Sister Meg Funk, OSB, Our Lady of Grace Monastery, Beech Grove, Indiana

"Combining poetry, personal memories, and recollections of a retreat, Lucien Miller presents a vivid evocation of the late Japanese Dominican friar, Shigeto Vincent Oshida. Embodying values of both the Zen and the Catholic traditions in his spiritual journey, Oshida offered an inspiring and prayerful witness of simplicity, poverty, solitude, and concern for a world of suffering. This moving and loving portrait is highly recommended for all spiritual seekers."

> — Leo D. Lefebure, past president of the Society for Buddhist-Christian Studies, and chair of theology, Georgetown University

"Shigeto Vincent Oshida was a saint, a mystic, a Christian visionary, and a model of an authentic appropriation of Buddhist and Christian truths that collectively lead to a new vision of discipleship. Lucien Miller takes us deeply into the life and heart of Fr. Oshida whose existence was utterly simple and yet filled with paradoxes. He was a hermit in community, a solitary among others. He desired nothing other than to disappear into the silence and bear witness to the 'Unborn Sphere,' all the while in complete service to the poor and those seeking his spiritual guidance. Miller's book inspires and challenges us to see a new model of the Christian life no longer dominated by a 'Western' model, but one immersed in the spirit of Asia."

> — Peter Feldmeier, professor of Catholic Studies, University of Toledo, Ohio

"Shigeto Oshida's quest was to reveal the Christ indigenous to Japanese culture. Lucien Miller's generous account shows us how he did this by rooting himself in the eternal rhythms of mountainous, rural rice-farming Japan, practicing zazen, offering Mass in a simple thatched roof hut, and opening himself to whatever the moment might bring."

> — David Hackett, professor emeritus of Religion, University of Florida

MONASTIC INTERRELIGIOUS DIALOGUE SERIES

Jesus in the Hands of Buddha

The Life and Legacy of Shigeto Vincent Oshida, OP

Lucien Miller (signature)

Lucien Miller

Foreword
by
Timothy Radcliffe, OP

To our dear neighbor and my favorite Electrician Congratulations,

Philip (handwritten inscription)

LITURGICAL PRESS
Collegeville, Minnesota

www.litpress.org

Cover design by Monica Bokinskie.
Cover photo depicts sculpture by the late Heidemarie Kern.

Interior photographs produced by the late Anne Martens. Permissions granted by the Japanese Dominicans who oversee Takamori.

1	2	3	4	5	6	7	8	9

Library of Congress Cataloging-in-Publication Data

Names: Miller, Lucien, author. | Radcliffe, Timothy, writer of foreword.
Title: Jesus in the hands of Buddha : the life and legacy of Shigeto Vincent Oshida, OP / Lucien Miller.
Description: Collegeville, Minnesota : Liturgical Press, [2023] | Series: Monastic interreligious dialogue series | Includes bibliographical references. | Summary: "A memoir of Father Shigeto Oshida, a man who was at once a Japanese Zen Buddhist Master and a Catholic Dominican priest"— Provided by publisher.
Identifiers: LCCN 2022046139 (print) | LCCN 2022046140 (ebook) | ISBN 9780814668672 (trade paperback) | ISBN 9780814669365 (library-only) | ISBN 9780814668689 (epub) | ISBN 9780814668689 (pdf)
Subjects: LCSH: Oshida, Shigeto, 1922– | Dominicans—Japan—Biography. | Zen Buddhists—Japan—Biography. | Priests—Japan—Biography. | Buddhism—Relations—Christianity. | Christianity and other religions—Buddhism.
Classification: LCC BX4705.O7335 M55 2023 (print) | LCC BX4705.O7335 (ebook) | DDC 294.3092 [B]—dc23/eng/20221115
LC record available at https://lccn.loc.gov/2022046139
LC ebook record available at https://lccn.loc.gov/2022046140

To

Anne Martens: Soulmate in Christ (1945–2022)

Chisato Kitagawa: Spiritual Guide and
Master in All Things Japanese (1932–2022)

John Deeney: Godfather of Chinese-Western
Comparative Literature (1931–2022)

Three who lived for others

CONTENTS

Jesus in the
Hands of Buddha Sculpture

The cover of this book portrays a unique image of Buddha and Jesus, truly iconic for those devoted to the encounter between contemplative spiritualities East and West.

Next to the gravesite of Father Shigeto Oshida in the woods of his hermitage, Takamori Soan, there is a one-foot-high clay sculpture made by the late Heidemarie Kern of the Child Jesus being held by Amida Buddha. "The idea of the sculpture," Heidemarie wrote, "just came out of me."[1] The Child, with arms outstretched before the cross, stands on a ball that rests on the palms of Amida's hands and is secured by his thumbs. Catholics might be moved to imagine the Infant of Prague with its traditional *globus cruciger* (orb and cross).

When I look at this icon, I see the Buddha basking in the Real Presence. The Amida Buddha of all-embracing love, his face radiating innocence and serenity, compassion and awareness, blissfully holds the Child Jesus in the mudra of deep contemplation. He protects and adores the Child who stands

---

[1] Heidemarie Kern email to Lucien Miller, May 18, 2015. Heidemarie Kern was a German Catholic nurse who went to Japan to practice zazen under Yamada Koun Roshi (山田耕雲), visited Father Oshida, and stayed several times at Takamori Soan. A member and teacher in the Bodhisangha interfaith community in India, she devoted her life to assisting the dying. She died in India in 2021.

before the cross, knowing full well who he is, what he has done, and what he will do. He is Son of Mary and Son of God who suffered and died for us. He is the Word and Heart of God poured out in redemptive love for the whole world.

According to my friend, the late Chisato Kitagawa, Episcopal priest and professor of Japanese at the University of Massachusetts at Amherst,

> The Buddha-Jesus statue at Takamori Soan symbolizes the dynamic of eternal salvation so well. Buddha, in a sense, is the Lord of this world. There is a story about Buddha saying at his birth, "I alone am the honored one in the heavens and on earth" (Chinese 天上天下唯我独尊). Jesus is the Son of the Holy Other, the Father, who is not contained in this universe, but is its Creator. Jesus is sent to live among us in this world as a channel for eternal salvation. Buddha, gazing upon the child, Jesus, is holding incarnate Love, coming from the Holy Other as His Only Son. Buddha represents this world, yearning for salvation.[2]

> Not Catholic doctrine, nor Buddhist teaching.
> Sub-Currents in our world?
> Word-Event born from the Unborn Sphere?

---

[2] Kitagawa in an email to me December 12, 2018.

FOREWORD

I stayed for a couple of days with my Dominican brother Shigeto Oshida in Takamori Soan in the late nineties, when, as master of the order, I was visiting the Dominican family in Japan. He took me to see the statue of the Buddha holding the child Jesus, and the little spring flowing from the rock into three rivulets. It was cold at night and the little thatched cottage in which I slept had no heating, and so he told me to lie on a mattress with the hot water jar while with much laughter and merriment, he covered me with so many layers of blankets that I wondered how I would ever get out!

In the morning, he presided at an exquisitely simple celebration of the Mass in the tiny chapel. On the altar was one of the images of Christ on which Christians were required to trample if they were to avoid torture and death during the persecutions of the faith in the early seventeenth century. This was a direct link to the first Dominicans to come to Japan, many of whom were martyred because they refused to do so. Oshida also bore in his heart those first Christians who did not hold out.

My memory above all is of an *encounter* with this extraordinary person, his profound joy and simplicity. He was unlike anyone whom I had ever met before, a Zen master, a Buddhist who had met Jesus, a Dominican friar, and a Catholic priest. Yet I felt utterly at home with him, touched at the core of my being.

This book by Lucien Miller is for me a sort of reliving and deepening of that encounter. I found myself invited to live again the joy of that moment and Oshida's challenging invitation to renew my faith and to embrace my life as a Christian at a deeper level. I hope that those who read this book will experience—a key word for Oshida—something of the unsettling beauty of that meeting, in which one is embraced without reserve and invited to venture further into the mystery.

I confess willingly that sometimes I am puzzled by Oshida. Lucien's book is authentic because he is unashamed to confess his own bewilderment at times. If I was at times thrown by Oshida's statements or way of being, this is not because of a lack of clarity, as if all could be made clear with a few simple statements. The challenge is far more profound. He was a living koan who invited one to see the world anew and in a way that could not be reduced to the categories in which Westerners like myself habitually think. There are some insights into which one can only be shocked! This is not unlike the way that Jesus' parables work. They do not explain or illustrate his teaching. They are like fireworks that explode in the night sky, casting a new light on who we are and what we live. "Look again!" they say.

Every encounter with the One who has become flesh and blood with us in Jesus will disrupt our old certainties. God's mystery can never be caught in flat literalism, which is why Christianity is always in need of poets and artists to open doorways into the transcendent. But Iain McGilchrist, in a groundbreaking book, *The Master and His Emissary*,[1] argued that in this historical moment, Western culture is often impoverished by the dominance of a way of thinking that is drily analytical, narrowed by reductionism and abstraction. It is ill at ease with ambiguity and metaphor. It settles for either/or rather than both/and. McGilchrist hopes that an encounter with Oriental culture can awaken us from this imaginative impoverishment and open our eyes to see the world anew.

---

[1] *The Master and His Emissary: The Divided Brain and the Making of the Western World*, new exp. ed. (New Haven and London: Yale University Press, 2019).

He claims that in Zen Buddhism, according to Soiku Shige-matasu, the abbot of Shogenji temple,

> a word is a finger that points at the moon. The goal of Zen pupils is the moon itself, not the pointing finger. Zen masters, therefore, will never stop cursing words and letters. In general, the Japanese place far more emphasis on individual existing things than on generalities, are more intuitive, and less cognitive, when compared with Westerners, and are not so easily swayed by logic and system building.[2]

When I read that, I thought immediately: Yes! This is Oshida!

No wonder that Christianity is often perceived as boring by our contemporaries and even unspiritual. Our faith invites us to *metanoia*, a Greek word usually translated as "repentance" but that means a transformation of how one sees the world. Especially in this historical moment, a Japanese Christian such as Oshida offers us an invitation not just to deepen our understanding of our faith but to challenge our Western culture. So, when Oshida says something that may seem nonsensical to us, we need to abide with our puzzlement, and wait for the moment when we may glimpse his meaning. When Oshida said, "Look at this flower. It is Jesus," instead of dismissing it, "How silly," I am beginning to learn to dwell with the statement. "Dwell" and "abide" are words that are at the core of the theology of John's gospel, which was so loved by Oshida. With expectant attention, we await the dawn of understanding.

It was Oshida's vocation, and sometimes his pain, to live the tension between the Western form of religious life, which he embraced when he became a Dominican, and his Zen Buddhism. He loved the church but was angry with its limited vision and its betrayal of the mystery. Yet he had the courage to abide in it as his home, and the order had the courage to accept this brother whom often they could not understand.

---

[2] McGilchrist, *Master and His Emissary*, 452f.

When he said to his local superior in Japan, the Canadian Father Bernard Trahan, that he wished to leave the community to live as a hermit, Bernard confessed that he did not like or understand this proposal, "but I have no right to prevent you from doing so. Please, Father, go ahead with your plan freely." What courage Bernard showed in opening the order to what he could not personally understand. In a sense, this is the challenge of this book for us all.

I would like, though, to share a few clues as to what helps me to glimpse the meaning of my encounter with Oshida and his teaching. It is not intended to reinterpret his teaching in more familiar terms. That would be to subvert the purpose of this book, which is to invite us to move beyond them. It is merely to share some of my experience of how he has touched me, both in that stay in Takamori and also in pondering on this fascinating book. This may or may not be useful for you.

As I stated earlier, in these pages I relived, even more deeply, my meeting with my brother Oshida in his home in the Japanese Alps. I was touched by his humanity, his humor and vitality, also sensing the pain and suffering he had endured. This encounter opened the door to the hidden center of his being, the encounter with God in Jesus. For Oshida, it is the experience, the encounter, that unlocks insight.

When we meet someone, do we *really* encounter anyone in their gritty particularity, or do two surfaces politely or aggressively bounce off each other? For Oshida everything was grounded in a true encounter with the other. Then one might glimpse the Divine Other. Once, when he was staying in a posh country club in America, he went for a walk in the woods. "Suddenly I had a strange feeling that someone was hurrying after me. As I turned to look over my shoulder, an old man began to speak to me without any word of introduction. 'Won't you please come to my house for a brief visit?' " This was the famous Hungarian artist and woodcutter, Joseph Domjan. Each was utterly rooted in their own traditions, but it was a meeting that transformed them both. "The phoenix spread its wings wide above."

Father James Campbell, an American Dominican, loved to tell of his meeting with Oshida. He had been a bomber pilot in the Second World War and repented of his collusion in this violence. He went to Japan to ask for forgiveness and there met Oshida. James expressed his sorrow at his sin; Oshida laughed and said that he had been in the anti-aircraft artillery and he repented that he had not shot down James! There followed laughter and the tumbling down of all barriers. Two people face-to-face, naked and unafraid.

Similarly, any encounter with the Word of God is not primarily the transmission of information. It is a Word-Event. Exactly as McGilchrist would lead us to expect, Oshida had a profound distrust of abstract language, which he refers to as "the third leg of the chicken," a leg that does not exist in reality, a conceptual construct. I had already encountered his rejection of the third leg but Lucien introduced me to Oshida's horror of the Parrot-Word, which is the mechanical repetition of language, and the Black-and-White Word, which excludes all ambiguity, all tension, imprisoning one in the anemic, univocal, polarizing categories so typical of Western contemporary culture. These are words that barricade one against the life-giving encounter with another, and with the Eternal Word that addresses me.

Oshida so rightly rejects most preaching as vacuous. "Anyone can give a sermon. In church there is no Word-Event. No life. People prefer Columbo," referring to the detective hero of a popular TV series. Our words about the Word of life must be ignited by an encounter with the Living God.

Cornelius Ernst, OP, was a Sri Lankan Dominican who was born just two years after Oshida. His father was a Dutch Protestant Christian and his mother a Buddhist, and so he bore in his own being something of the tension that animated Oshida. Cornelius too was a convert to Catholicism, becoming so when he was in Cambridge as a student of the philosopher Wittgenstein. He believed that grace worked in our lives through its creative fertility, what he called "the genetic moment":

Every genetic moment is a mystery. It is dawn, discovery, spring, new birth, coming to the light, awakening, transcendence, liberation, ecstasy, bridal consent, gift, forgiveness, reconciliation, revolution, faith, hope, love. It could be said that Christianity is the consecration of the genetic moment, the living centre from which it reviews the indefinitely various and shifting perspectives of human experience in history. That, at least, is or ought to be its claim: that it is the power to transform and renew all things: "Behold, I make all things new."[3]

All those touched by the mystery of God know that our words only speak when they provoke the event of grace in our lives. In *Peace like a River*, a novel by an American called Leif Enger, a young kid asks about a preacher, "Do things happen, when he preaches"?[4] Usually, not much! A fifteenth-century Sufi imam, Mullah Nasrudin, is supposed to have said, "I talk all day, but when I see someone's eyes blaze, then I write it down." The Hebrew word for "word" means also "an event," as does the Japanese word *koto*.

This encounter for Oshida was often described as "the Hand of God," touching our inmost being, culminating in the Christ who touched the sick and whose pierced hands were stretched out on the cross. This is why he did not like the usual translation of the beginning of John's gospel, "In the beginning was the Word." He would say, "In the beginning was the Hand."

How can we become open to the Event of God in our lives? Without this, all our words will be worthless. Each of us must follow our own path but, if I have understood him correctly, some clues reoccur often in Oshida's writings.

The first task, as surely in all the major religions, is to be liberated from the arrogance of the ego. This is that self-absorption that becomes a barrier between us and each other and all of reality, the hungry, grasping, manipulative self. It is,

---

[3] *The Theology of Grace* (Notre Dame, IN: Fides Publishers, 1974), 74f.
[4] *Peace like a River* (New York: Atlantic Monthly Press, 2001), 28.

Oshida believed, a particular temptation for religious people. People may fall into thinking how good they are! He became aware of its prison when he was a Dominican in the first years of formation:

> I felt I had wasted all my life. At that moment I saw all my past and I remembered, for example, how I would not eat but distributed food door to door. It was my passion: my zealous emotion. It was not by the Holy Spirit. It was my halo. I received an arrow in my chest. I tasted what ego is, arrogance. Since then, the spiritual life became a promenade with the hands in the pockets—to get free of the smell of ego.

How is one to become free of its blinders? One cannot think one's way out of its entrapment for then one may be plunged into self-consciousnessly trying to become unself-conscious! For Oshida, his frequent experiences of sickness and of his brushes with death were his guru. "The Master of my Zen, my guru," he once remarked, "was my sickness." In his experiences of tuberculosis, he was confronted with his fragility, his dependence on the Hand of God. Each breath was a struggle; each breath was a gift, "when you experience helplessness, forgiveness, and freedom. Like a vulnerable bug on its back— flailing its legs in powerlessness. Eventually the bug is set aright—but not by its own power alone—then flies away, free to be itself."

Personally, I found this immensely helpful. I have been living with cancer of the mouth and then of the jaw on and off for the last six years. Who knows what comes next? Faced with sickness, our language is so often violent and combative. One must "fight" against this cancer; it must be "beaten"! Oshida invites me to see my situation otherwise. My own experiences of cancer can be my guru too, opening my eyes to the gift of every day, and the Giver of every gift.

During Oshida's sickness and convalescence in the sanatorium in Sendai, he discovered a new community. Lucien writes,

"Oshida believed that his vision for Takamori began with his profound experience of a *madoi* (円居), a 'living friendship circle' of people at Sendai. It was made up of patients with whom he bonded during their hospitalization." Here he learnt simplicity, "to be simple within ourselves in order to be open to God." When he talked to an official about the foundation of Takamori, he said, "I want to start a *madoi* of God in this area where poor people can live together." Living with the poor, becoming simple, heals one of the smell of the ego and so opens one to the happening of the Word of God, the Hand that reaches out with its healing touch.

One's ultimate poverty is revealed when one awakes to one's mortality, and Oshida almost died three times. Then we know in truth that, as Psalm 144 says, we are only a breath and our life is but a fleeting shadow. We treasure our lives and all of creation, suspended over nothingness. We are most aware of the pure gift of everything when our eyes are open to its transience. This again, McGilchrist believes, is at the heart of much Japanese art and religion: "The impermanence of nature (*shizen*) is seen as the Buddhahood, or essence of the divine. In the West, with our recording apparatus of every kind, we value what we can grasp and hold. But life and everything living refuses this approach. It changes as we hold it."[5] In the West we have often valued what is immutable, unchanging. So here, embracing his sickness and death, we see Oshida as indeed the Buddhist who has encountered Christ. There is a reconciliation but it is not on the conceptual level. It is ontological, in his very being.

If we can but open our eyes, liberate our sight from the blinders of the grasping ego, we will see things, listen to them, and learn from them. Hence the importance for Oshida of manual work, the naked encounter with our world. The rice fields around Takamori were places of beauty and education.

[5] McGilchrist, *Master and His Emissary*, 453.

When Oshida gave retreats, especially for bishops used to the sedentary life, he enjoyed sending them to plant rice in the paddy fields, impervious to their protests about backaches. He wrote, "A farmer who works hard from dawn to dusk knows that a grain of rice is not his product, a thing made by his own effort, but something given to him by God. He must offer the grain of rice to God who is hidden but who gives everything. He must say 'This is yours.'"[6]

Lucien describes with typical modesty his own struggle to work in the rice fields. I am glad that I did not stay long enough for Oshida to invite me to work in them! Yet here one learns, he believed, to see and to listen. "Listen to the rice. Be the farmer. The farmer listens. The rice tells him when it wants to be planted, fertilized, weeded, and harvested. How it should be cut and stacked. He doesn't read it out of a book. Listen, listen, listen. The rice will tell you everything."

Oshida describes the art of seeing as learning "the faraway look." One sees both the transient particular, but also the whole. "When you look into another's eyes, see the whole person—the baby, the old man, the young girl. Experience unity. Now you will know what charity is. If you live in a state of *dhyana*, deep contemplation, you always have the faraway look." You see the single grain of rice and the interconnectedness of all things. He delighted to see this binocular vision exemplified in a footballer such as the Brazilian Pelé, who must see every detail on the pitch and yet the interconnectedness of everything. He had the "faraway look"!

The fruit of this liberation from the ego and the encounter with the Lord is joy. Joy, he said, "is not something to explain but to experience." All who met Oshida were touched by overflowing, bubbling merriment, his almost childlike joy. I remember his joy as he tucked me up in bed in the chilly guest room, the same joy that overflowed in the retreats that Lucien de-

---

[6] Claudia Mattiello, *Takamori Sōan: Teachings of Shigeto Oshida, a Zen Master* (Buenos Aires: Talleres Gráficos Color Efe, 2007), 75.

scribes, his irrepressible sense of fun. He even rejoiced in God's tricking him into becoming a Christian since he was fooled into thinking that every Christian would be like the marvelous first priest whom he encountered, or into being a Dominican, before discovering that most Dominicans were not the mystics he had expected. It was joy that triumphed in his life, even to the end. His last words were, "God is wonderful. God is wonderful, God is wonderful. Amen. Amen. Amen. Amen!"

Timothy Radcliffe, OP
Master of the Order of Preachers, 1992–2001
August 6, 2022
Feast of the Transfiguration
77th anniversary of the atomic bombing of Hiroshima

INTRODUCTION

I am the way, and the truth, and the life. (John 14:6)

Come to me, all you that are weary and
are carrying heavy burdens,
and I will give you rest. (Matt 11:28)

Look within. Be still.
Free from fear and attachment,
know the sweet joy of the way. (Dhammapada)

My initial encounter with Father Shigeto Oshida seems to have been a matter of the movement of the stars. In the spring of 1976, after a sabbatical in Taiwan and just one week before I was to return to the United States with my wife and three little children, I happened upon a tattered poster on a telephone pole announcing a weeklong Christian-Zen retreat. It was to be directed by William Johnston, SJ, an Irish Jesuit theologian teaching at Sophia University in Tokyo who was widely honored for his major contributions to the development of Buddhist-Christian encounter. I immediately decided to take part in the retreat. Given that my wife and I had so little time to prepare for our departure from Taiwan, it was a rash, even foolish, decision, but it was one I simply had to make.[1]

---

[1] For my essay on Father Johnston's retreat, see Lucien Miller, "Wisdom's Flowering Cherry Tree: The Charismatic Zen of William Johnston, SJ," *Dilatato Corde* 11, no. 2 (2021), https://dimmid.org/index.asp?Type=B_BASIC&SEC =%7b79A59B4F-013C-4E0D-B86B-80D28C12A258%7d. The essay also appears

At the retreat's end, Father Johnston said that if I were really interested in Christian-Zen, I had to go to Japan and spend some time with Father Shigeto Oshida at his Takamori Hermitage in the Japanese Alps. Once again a silent "yes" straight away flashed through my mind. Though there was no time to obtain a Japanese visa, something deep within was drawing me inexorably to Father Oshida. I immediately decided I would jump ship during a stopover in Tokyo and somehow make my way to Father Oshida's Takamori Hermitage in the Japanese Alps. Thank God, my precious family graciously agreed to head home to San Francisco without me.

With this memoir of my providential encounter with that amazing Zen master, Dominican priest and hermit, and founder of the Takamori Hermitage in the Japanese Alps,[2] I want to invite readers to enter their own journey to Jesus in the hands of Buddha. The common ground and unifying thread is grace—the unmitigated gift of divine love that permeates individuals, events, and locations and makes them holy.

In chapter 1 of this memoir, "A Buddhist Who Encountered Christ," I provide a brief biography of Father Oshida, who, like Jeremiah, felt he was duped by God into becoming a Catholic, a Dominican, and a priest and who, as a Christian-Buddhist hermit, eventually founded an international interfaith community in Japan. The core of this book consists of chapters on Father Oshida's Takamori Hermitage, his Christian-Zen teaching, his contemplative retreats (*sesshin*), and his impact on me as well as countless individuals, vowed religious and lay, all over the globe. In an epilogue we join a small international interfaith community of Christians and Buddhists for a joyous celebration of his life and legacy.

---

in *Buddhist-Christian Studies* 42 (2022) with the title "Wisdom's Flowering Cherry: William Johnston's Charismatic Zen."

[2] Portions of this memoir were previously published in *The Hidden Side of the Mountain: Encounters with Wisdom's Poor and Holy* (Louisville, KY: Fons Vitae, 2021).

Should you feel hesitant about reading a book like this because of your concern that your faith will be weakened or even destroyed by too much exposure to philosophical systems or spiritual beliefs and practices that are not only different from but even appear to be opposed to yours, an introductory word about Father Oshida's own experience of reconciling his Buddhist background and his Catholic faith might entice you to read on.

If you thumb your way forward you will note that as he recounts how he, as a Buddhist, came to discover Jesus, he cannot help thinking that God tricked him. Like the Jewish prophet Jeremiah who felt he had been seduced by God (see Jer 20:7), Oshida felt God had deceived him—and not only once but three times! Encountering the person of Christ embodied in a Catholic foreign missionary, he immediately longed to be baptized. After his baptism, he discovered to his dismay that most Catholics were not at all like that missionary. Subsequently, a Jesuit spiritual adviser inspired him to become a priest, but it did not take long for him to ascertain that most priests had very little of the charisma of his mentor. Finally, a Dominican mystic enkindled in him the desire to become a Dominican friar. During his novitiate and seminary years he awoke to the realization that most friars were not mystics.

Through all the twists and turns of his spiritual journey, Oshida remained convinced that to follow Jesus he did not have to stop being a Buddhist. He never doubted that it was not only possible, but also necessary for him to reconcile his love of Jesus with the Buddhist wisdom that had so profoundly shaped his understanding of what it is to be human. His conviction resonates with that of my mentor and guide in this endeavor, the late Trappist monk Thomas Merton (1915–1968). In a talk he gave in Bangkok shortly before his death on December 10, 1968, he said,

> I believe that by openness to Buddhism, to Hinduism, and to these great Asian traditions, we stand a wonderful chance of learning more about the potentiality of our own

traditions, because they have gone, from the natural point of view, so much deeper into this than we have. The combination of the natural techniques and the graces and the other things that have been manifested in Asia and the Christian liberty of the gospel should bring us all at last to that full and transcendent liberty which is beyond mere cultural differences and mere externals—and mere this or that.[3]

Throughout his spiritual journey Oshida emphasized direct spiritual experience as the means to bring about this reconciliation. May your coming to know this remarkable spiritual seeker, whose love for Jesus was profoundly enhanced by the richness of Buddhist wisdom and insight, help you to reconcile spiritual paths that seem to be opposed and thus come to experience the fruits of cross-cultural Buddhist-Christian engagement.[4] "This fire will pass from heart to heart," Father Oshida prophesied. "Respect the mystery of each faith."

Before his sudden death in 1968, Merton began to acquaint himself with several different Asian spiritual traditions. The one I interiorized and wish to explore with the reader is Buddhist, specifically the contemplative path of Zen Buddhism. It is a grand aspiration, perhaps too grand for me, but hopefully my Christian-Zen pilgrimage will touch you if you are a beginner in the field of interreligious encounters or will encourage you to deepen your encounter with another spiritual tradition that is already well underway. My deepest hope, as you interiorize Father Oshida's way of experiential prayer and gaze

---

[3] *The Asian Journal of Thomas Merton*, ed. Naomi Burton, Brother Patrick Hart, and James Laughlin (New York: New Directions Books, 1973, 1975), 343.

[4] Robert Magliola has authored a book approaching Buddhist-Christian encounter in a way differing from what I am exploring here, but which I recommend for those dialoguing with all three vehicles of Buddhism—Theravada, Mahayana, and Vajrayana. *Facing Up to Real Doctrinal Difference: How Some Thought-Motifs from Derrida Can Nourish the Catholic-Buddhist Encounter* (Kettering, OH: Angelico Press, 2014).

upon Jesus in the hands of Buddha, is that you taste the fruits of interreligious dialogue and spiritual practice.

In an Advent sermon, the twelfth-century Cistercian Abbot Guerric of Igny (c.1070/80–1157) said, "Let us hear what the Voice of the Word calls to us, so that one day we may progress from the Voice to the Word."[5] Guided by the Holy Spirit, imbued with the wisdom of the Buddha, blessed by the Holy Innocents of Asia and America—the rejected and forgotten *anawim* whom Father Oshida so loved—may we all give ear to his voice and progress from the voice to the Word.

---

[5] "Iterim tamen quod vox Verbi nobis clamat audiamus, ut quandoque de voce ad Verbum proficiamus." John Morson and Hilary Costello, *Guerric d'Igny: Sermons*, 2 vols., *Sources Chrétiennes* (Paris: Cerf, 1970, 1973), vol. 166, p. 138.

CHAPTER ONE

A Buddhist Who Encountered Christ

For Shigeto Vincent Oshida, Buddhism was the home within him that became a dwelling place for Christ. This Japanese Dominican priest, who died in 2003 at the age of eighty-one, was a Buddhist-Christian mystic who longed to be a hermit but was called to become the founder and director of an international interfaith center that was visited by thousands of spiritual seekers from around the world.

My sketch of Father Oshida's life and interreligious faith journey is essentially personal. There are a few books and articles about him to which I will refer, especially Claudia Mattiello's excellent summary of his teachings.[1] In a thirty-three minute video of an interview with Father Oshida conducted by Lucette Verboven, his deep and vibrant spirituality is strikingly displayed.[2] I rely mainly on my encounters with him at his Takamori Hermitage (*soan*) in the Japanese Alps, my participation in *sesshins* (contemplative retreats) he directed in the United States, and the "contemplative breakfasts" I had with my late colleague and dear friend, Chisato Kitagawa, one of the three persons to whom this book is dedicated. Father Kitagawa was my spiritual mentor as well as the wellspring

---

[1] *Takamori Sōan: Teachings of Shigeto Oshida, a Zen Master* (Buenos Aires: Talleres Gráficos Color Efe, 2007; first edition in Spanish, 2005). This and other publications on or by Oshida are included in the bibliography. For a detailed, chronological outline of his life and publications, see "Vita" at the end of this volume.

[2] Available on YouTube. Search for it with "Lucette Verboven Oshida."

of my understanding of everything Japanese related to Father Oshida: language, literature, culture, and customs. Moreover, it was Chisato's intuitive grasp of the preeminence of the poor in the ministry of Christ that brought me to a deeper understanding and embrace of Father Oshida's love for the *anawim*, the Holy Innocents of the world who suffer through no fault of their own.

For several years Chisato and I met at a restaurant in Amherst for bimonthly discussions about Father Oshida and about the place of poverty and suffering in the spiritual life of Christians. One morning Chisato shared a dream. I cite it to reveal how his friendship and guiding spirit sustained and encouraged me in a way that is beyond my telling.

> You are on your way to Bethlehem, one of the Three Wise Men, to see the baby Jesus, guided by the light of two stars, Thomas Merton and Shigeto Oshida. You discover the Holy Innocent, Christ, whose existence leads to the martyrdom of all boys in Bethlehem under the age of two. You do not know what to do about the Holy Innocents whom you will stumble upon, "by accident"—how to understand them. You do not yet know them—the victims, the poor, to whom you will awake on your pilgrimage, East and West, the aborted Yet-to-be-Born, the hapless women hod and brick and coffee sack carriers, the road builders smashing rocks by hand, the sunken eyes of lepers missing hands, toes, and noses, the dying innocents in Mother Teresa's houses of hospitality—these are the Holy Innocents. You did not become "enlightened," aware, awakened, until you realized they were Jesus, the scapegoat, upon whose innocence the world heaps its sins, the sins it cannot confess, for to do so might destroy it.

Chisato's dream inspired me to complete a book I was writing on the spirituality of the poor in India and China.[3] His

---

[3] Lucien Miller, *The Hidden Side of the Mountain: Encounters with Wisdom's Poor and Holy* (Louisville, KY: Fons Vitae, 2021).

constant insights and cheering presence guided my writing of this memoir of Shigeto Oshida.

This chapter is by no means a complete and definitive portrayal of the life and ministry of Father Oshida. Rather, it focuses on the period between his conversion to Catholicism and his founding of Takamori Soan.[4] Father Oshida's own understanding of Takamori, its beginnings and meaning, its way of life and appeal, is especially illuminating, for it contextualizes his interior call to live as a hermit in community while remaining dedicated to his vocation as a Catholic priest and a Dominican who continued to be a Buddhist. In his eyes, Takamori was the flowering of his priesthood in the Order of Preachers. From my viewpoint, the origins of Takamori are mysteriously providential, a combination of chance encounter and personal illness. His vocation came from a similar fortuitous intersection of his unique personality with circumstance, historical context, and grace.

Tricked by God

In 1943, a few months prior to his being drafted into the Japanese army, Oshida had an extraordinary encounter with a Catholic priest. Like other high school and college students of that era, he had learned about Christianity, but he had no interest in the Christian faith or way of life. One day, he happened to drop by a Catholic church in the Tokyo neighborhood of Kōjimachi, and there he discovered Christ in the person of Father Herman Heuvers (1890–1977), a German Jesuit who had been the president of Tokyo's Sophia University from 1937 to 1941.

---

[4] Biographical details are gleaned from Oshida: "The Good News from Sinanosakai," 1965; English translation made after his death, unpublished manuscript; "Evangelization and Inculturation," *Tooi Manazashi, A Far Away Look*, English translation by Chisato Kitagawa (Tokyo: Chiyūsha, 1983); Rev. Chiemi Ishii Sasaki, "Encounter with Takamori—Encounter with the Deep Stream," unpublished manuscript; *sesshin* talks in America (see chaps. 4 and 5). See bibliography for works by and about Oshida.

Oshida was immediately aware that he was meeting some-one truly exceptional. Indeed, so widely revered and respected was Heuvers that when he died, over 2,500 people attended his funeral. Since his encounter with this Catholic priest was so fortuitous and made such a strong impression on him, Oshida felt that "Catholicism" was something he could no longer ignore; he therefore soon asked to be baptized. As he was about to be inducted into the army, he received the sacrament knowing that he might soon die in combat. He was firmly resolved to accept that possibility or whatever else might happen to him during the war.

Many years later during a *sesshin* he led in the United States of America, Father Oshida remarked that he had become a Catholic "by a joke or trick of God," because he had assumed that all Catholics must be like this German Jesuit. The "trick of God," was a reference to the words of the prophet Jeremiah who suffered imprisonment and beatings for chastising his fellow Jews for their idolatry and faithlessness and who cried out,

> You seduced me, LORD, and I let myself be seduced;
> you were too strong for me, and you prevailed.
> All day long I am an object of laughter;
> everyone mocks me (Jer 20:7).

In Oshida's case, it was he who laughed; the joke was on him. God had seduced him, and he let himself be seduced into believing that all Catholics were like Father Heuvers.

Nonetheless, thanks to Father Heuvers, his disappointment did not keep him from pursuing his spiritual journey.

During the American Occupation of Japan (1945–1952), Oshida was an undergraduate student in the Philosophy Department at Tokyo University. He graduated in 1951 with a bachelor's degree in Indian philosophy. While still a student, he returned to Father Heuvers, telling him that he had explored various monastic communities but was undecided about his future course. It had occurred to him that he might like to visit the Dominican monastery in Sendai, north of Tokyo. He had come to believe that Dominicans were very explicit about seeing things from God's perspective rather than from a simply human point of view, and so he wondered if the window to his future might be opened there.

Oshida was not in the least prepared to hear the response of his spiritual director. He knew from others and through his own experience that Father Heuvers was extremely cautious about telling others what they should decide. Normally, he would say things like "Wait a while," counselling patience and further discernment. However, his words to Oshida were clear and direct: "It is clear that you are called. You have a vocation. There is no doubt about it."

Oshida was shocked when he heard this and initially resisted what sounded to him like a karmic final verdict in a court of law.

Father Heuvers went on to caution Oshida, telling him that his monastic vocation would not be easy for him. "The truth is, you have too much love for humanity to live an ordinary monastic life," he said. "Yet, it is even more true that the goal you set for yourself is too high to be a married man and have your own family."

"My life was decided by his words," Oshida said. Although he did not know it at the time, he was destined to follow a way of life that was altogether different from the regular conventual life of Dominican friars.

Drowning and *Madoi*—the Roots of Community

While an undergraduate, something else happened to Oshida that was transformative, both for himself and eventually for the circle of seekers who would gather around him. One day while swimming in turbulent waters at Arahama beach in Miyagi Prefecture he nearly drowned. An American soldier serving in the Occupation Armed Forces happened by and saved him. Oshida's mouth was so tightly clenched that the soldier had to use an iron bar to open it in order to apply artificial respiration. Oshida vividly recalled how close he had come to death and then been reborn, describing his experience of beginning to breathe again as "taking my first breath."

The date was August 12, 1948. Oshida was twenty-six years old. The immutable physical and mental marks of his near-death experience would stay with him until the day he died.

What marks?

During the war, army physicians discovered that he had tuberculosis. They determined he should be hospitalized, but he refused treatment. To my knowledge he never explained why. Surely he had deep empathy for his fellow soldiers. He once remarked, "Always in war it is the best boy who goes," meaning who goes to his death. He abhorred privilege. His ideal was Jesus. He wanted to be poor and live among the poor, his hands in his pocket and a whistle on his lips, as he would say, to be one with those for whom there is no room. Here I see a possible seed of his Dominican vocation and his attraction to the Dominican vow of voluntary evangelical poverty which he lived out at Takamori Soan in the Japanese Alps.

Later, when he almost drowned to death, his tuberculosis worsened, and he suffered gangrene of the lungs. Thus began his lifelong struggle with respiratory and lung illnesses. "The Master of my Zen, my guru," he once remarked, "was my sickness."[5] In "The Good News from Sinanosakai," a reminiscence Oshida recorded in 1965, he revealed that his "Master Sickness" was an unremitting thorn stuck in his side, constantly reminding him that he got to live while other TB patients did not:

---

[5] Shigeto Oshida, "The Mystery of the Word and the Reality," in *Toward a New Age in Mission: The Good News of God's Kingdom; To the Peoples of Asia*, International Congress on Mission, Manila, December 2–7, 1979, vol. 2, book 3 (Manila: Theological Conference Office, 1981), 210.

I know now that my lung disease will not heal and I want to confess that during all my life, I will take with me the debt that I owe to the patients of tuberculosis. Seventeen years ago [1948], I became very sick. It was a time in which medicines could hardly be obtained. I did survive due to the fact that, for my special position [perhaps as a former soldier], I obtained medicines, to which normal patients couldn't have access. I will never be able to forget the young man who was beside me at the hospital, a fisherman. He was dying then because he could not receive streptomycin. . . . He was operated on and died during the operation. [At that time, lung removal had become a treatment for tuberculosis in Japan]. I will never be able to forget his sharing of himself a few days before he died.[6]

After his near drowning in 1948, Father Oshida spent the next two years, off and on, recovering at Tohoku University Hospital in Sendai, the capital city of Miyagi Prefecture, and subsequently at the National Miyagi Prefectural Sanatorium in Sendai. This period of treatment was to be the first of many hospitalizations and recoveries at medical centers and tuberculosis sanitariums for years to come.

During his treatment at the Sendai sanatorium, Oshida did not forget Father Heuvers's conviction that he was being called to the religious life. To nurture his vocation, he attended Mass at Catholic churches in the Sendai area and at the Sendai Priory of the Order of Preachers, which had been founded by Canadian Dominicans. On Sundays, the US army would send a Jeep to take Catholics to these churches. Oshida accepted the rides yet felt hostile towards the American soldiers who were his former enemies.

Oshida was discharged from the Sendai sanatorium in 1950. Following graduation from Tokyo University in 1951, he formally entered the Dominicans, beginning his novitiate and taking his first (temporary) vows at the Sendai Priory. Inspired

---

[6] Oshida, "Good News from Sinanosakai."

by the novice master, Father Bernard Tarte, he made his final vows there in 1955.

During his years at the Sendai Priory (1951–1958), Oshida continued to suffer relapses of his lung disease and was in and out of hospitals and sanatoriums. A serious relapse occurred in 1952, for which he was hospitalized through 1953.

Oshida felt profoundly touched by the other TB patients he encountered at the hospital and sanatorium in Sendai and developed a deep sense of community with them. While none of these persons ever participated in the establishment and life of Takamori Soan, which began much later in 1964, Oshida believed that his vision for Takamori began with his profound experience of a *madoi* (円居), a "living friendship circle" of people at Sendai.[7] It was made up of patients with whom he bonded during their hospitalization. The seeds of the living tree of Takamori, which began to grow visibly in the mid-1960s, had begun sprouting in the soil of Sendai in the years following the war.

Father Oshida maintained a permanent connection within this intimate circle of soulmates. He was deeply touched by the simple and unpretentious way the sick lived together while recovering from tuberculosis. He retained a deep reverence for his initial taste of an uncluttered life, which teaches us, said Oshida, "to be simple with ourselves in order to be open to God."[8]

More Tricks of God—Father Bernard Tarte, Mystic

As we have already noted, Oshida was, in fact, duped three times. Encountering the person of Jesus embodied in Father Heuvers, a Catholic foreign missionary, he immediately longed to be baptized. After his baptism, he discovered to his dismay that most Catholics were not at all like that missionary. Sub-

---

[7] Chisato Kitagawa translation from Oshida, *Tooi Manazashi*, 102, 105–6.
[8] Oshida, "Evangelization and Inculturation."

sequently, the priestly witness of Father Heuvers inspired him to become ordained, only to find that most priests fell far short of the stature of his charismatic mentor.

And then came the mystic, Father Bernard Tarte. It was he who enkindled in Oshida the desire to delve more deeply into Dominican spirituality. Father Tarte was Provincial Vicar of the Dominicans in Japan from 1947 to 1955. He became Friar Oshida's spiritual director during his last years at the Sendai Priory (1956–1958). Once again God was tricking Oshida into thinking that all Dominicans must be mystics, and that being a Dominican friar was the way he would be able to live his life in the company of mystics. Alas, during his novitiate and seminary years he awoke to the realization that most friars were not mystics. Just as all Catholics and all priests were not like Father Heuvers, all Dominicans were not like Father Tarte.

Be that as it may, Oshida was captivated.

To begin with, Tarte was an unconventional teacher and his views were refreshingly original. At the beginning of a teaching session one morning, the priest urged his friars to move beyond hostile inflexibility and dependency on the letter of the law and turn toward following the spirit of the law. Father Tarte explained:

> If you keep the rules, you are kept. You are protected. But that's all. You should not criticize those who do not keep the rules. There are times that the rules must be broken. That is when you need to love. Love supersedes everything.[9]

Father Tarte lived in a dimension all his own, distinct from the other friars, whether he was praying, having a meal, or speaking on the phone.

One night, during the Grand Silence that is observed through the night, something happened that none of the friars

---

[9] Oshida, "Evangelization and Inculturation."

could explain. They could hear the distinctive breeding call of the storied Japanese Bush Warbler, which during the daylight hours proclaims the arrival of spring throughout Japan, reverberating through the darkness of night:

"Hoo ho-ke-kyo!" "Hoo ho-ke-kyo!" "Hoo ho-ke-kyo!"

Not only was it not daytime; it was not spring. Oshida and other friars began opening windows and going onto balconies to listen to this miracle of nature. At last, Oshida made out a ghostly figure walking about the garden. It was Father Tarte, sounding the haunting refrain on a bird-whistle.

"This is the world of *kotohogi*" (言祝ぎ), Oshida said to himself, using the Japanese Shinto term meaning "celebration or praise of the sacred." Instantly this world was opened to Oshida and became palpable. Now he felt comfortable being at the monastery. As Chisato Kitagawa noted, "Father Tarte's child-like joy and singularity, completely unencumbered by the anxiety of daily life, must have opened for Oshida a new vista, a possibility of a blessed life."[10]

Every day during the novitiate at the Priory there were similar events and moments. It was the singular Father Tarte who taught Oshida the meaning of true penance. "You must mock yourself and look upon your star, the cross," he told him. Oshida interpreted this to mean that penance should take you out of your consciousness, out of phenomena. He experienced this removal or transformation in Father Tarte directly. One day he entered the chapel and saw Father Tarte praying alone. Wanting not to disrupt the novice master while at prayer, friar Oshida started to turn away silently.

"Only God and you are here!" Father Tarte boomed. "Why do you worry about me?"

Oshida felt as if he had been struck by a bolt of lightning that brought him to an overwhelming awareness of his own self-conscious ego.

---

[10] Chisato Kitagawa email to Lucien Miller, December 8, 2014.

One early morning during the Grand Silence everyone heard loud music coming from Father Tarte's room. Oshida peeked in his door and heard the Banana Boat Song "Day O!" being sung at full volume by Harry Belafonte on the novice master's record player.

Oshida was baffled by this utter contrast between required silence and prohibited sound. Then he realized that Father Tarte, who was known to have a hard time waking up in the morning, was totally unaware of the ear-splitting music or of Oshida. He had "that faraway look," Oshida said, a feeling for the whole, a look that was always proportionate to his awareness of the complete mystery of each human being. Father Tarte was entirely unconscious of anything else. Beholding "that faraway look" Oshida wept.

Father Tarte perceived that Oshida's near drowning had had a profound impact on him, making him aware of an afterlife and knowing that everything was in God's hands. "What you are tasting is what theology calls *sapientia*—wisdom," said Father Tarte. Years later in an interview Oshida recounted his interior awareness of God's presence:

> When I hear a birdsong, I feel the hereafter; I hear the deepest voice of God, not mingled with my own voice or the voice of society. The child Shigeto, the adult, and the old man are present here, inseparably bound to Him, sometimes touched by His presence. God's breath is always there.[11]

Ordination and Priesthood

Inspired by Father Tarte's mystical spirituality, Oshida decided to persevere with his Dominican studies and hold fast to his monastic vocation. Before he made his final vows at

---

[11] Lucette Verboven, ed., "Vincent Shigeto Oshida (Japan)," in *The Dominican Way* (London: Continuum, 2011), 192.

Sendai Priory in 1955, however, he asked Jesus in the Eucharist whether he should permanently commit himself to the Order of Preachers. He had been profoundly affected by his experience of the small simple community he had been part of during his time in a tuberculosis sanatorium in Sendai, the *madoi* referred to above. The simplicity of that living friendship circle of the sick had felt very natural to him. He realized that for himself "this simplicity is a *'sine qua non'* for complete openness to God."[12] While he intuited a personal truth—that he could not remain truly humble and unpretentious in the Dominican Order—he did not yet have a sense of an alternative path.

Another Japanese friar friend had the same question and told him about a conversation he had had with their common Jesuit spiritual director, Father Heuvers. Father Heuvers advised Oshida's friend that such questions about living a humble and simple spiritual life were too advanced for someone at his level of development. Oshida borrowed the advice Father Heuvers had given to his friend and stopped worrying—for the time being.

"Jesus did not answer my question," Oshida admitted wryly.[13]

His unanswered question together with his contemplative master—his sickness—continued to instruct him. "One way or another," he told an interviewer, "I survived in the conviction that I could not die and leave behind the church as a bastion of the conventional bourgeoisie! My ideal was the priesthood even if I could only say Mass once."[14]

In 1958 Oshida entered the Dominican Theological Seminary in Ottawa, Canada. There he learned French, the language of the Dominicum Studium or House of Studies. The works of

---

[12] "Evangelization and Inculturation," *Monastic Interreligious Dialogue Bulletin* 75, ed. Mark Delery (October 2005): 3–4.

[13] See chap. 5 below, "*Sesshin* Part Two."

[14] Verboven, "Vincent Shigeto Oshida (Japan)," 191.

St. Thomas Aquinas were read in Latin, but the lectures on them were given in French. While Oshida was an excellent student, he continued to feel that the Dominican monastic way of life was unnatural for him; it was too great a contrast to the Asian Wisdom path he knew. Since Jesus still did not answer his question or his fears, however, he struggled on.

Oshida's father was a Buddhist in the Soto Zen tradition, and Shigeto had grown up with a deep love of *zazen*. He and his father would do *zazen* together from the time he was in elementary school. He recalled that whenever *zazen* came up in the course of a conversation, his father would say, "Hey, let's sit."[15] It was through the practice of *zazen* that he survived his seminary years and held fast to his vocation. The superior of the Canadian Province of the Dominicans believed that Oshida's particular calling was to transplant the European or Canadian Dominican way of life to Japan, but Oshida thought otherwise. He told his superior that perhaps he could live that life himself in Japan, but he could never ask the younger generation of Japanese to do the same.[16]

Before his ordination on April 8, 1961, Oshida made a "promise to Him": "I shall not lie any more to myself and to You after the ordination."[17] I think he felt he was lying by not letting others know he felt smothered by the European cultural impact on Catholicism. From now on he would be clear about it, as he was when he asked his superior for permission to leave parish ministry and be on his own, seeking to follow God's will for him as a Japanese Dominican priest who was convinced that there had to be a Japanese—and indeed, a Buddhist—way of being a Catholic. Thus, when the time came for the reception of holy orders and someone wanted to honor the event by

[15] Oshida, *Tooi Manazashi*, 135. Chisato Kitagawa email to Lucien Miller, May 19, 2015.

[16] "Evangelization and Inculturation," *Monastic Interreligious Dialogue Bulletin*, 3–4.

[17] "Evangelization and Inculturation," *Monastic Interreligious Dialogue Bulletin*, 4.

giving Oshida money to purchase a new chalice, he simply could not bear the thought of having a metal chalice made and then plated with gold or silver, as required by church law at the time. "Anything plated with metal would be a symbol of a falsehood to a Japanese soul," he declared. "To me it would mean a mixing of worldly spirituality with religious spirituality." Besides, he knew that most of the world's gold came from South Africa where apartheid reigned. Instead, he had a chalice created, Japanese-style, out of powdered stone and fired at 1300 degrees. This chalice met with his inner need for simplicity. "Happily," Oshida said, "it was blessed by the papal nuncio in Japan" some years later.[18]

Oshida's tuberculosis worsened soon after ordination, and he was hospitalized yet again, this time at Hôpital Maisonneuve Montreal and then at a convalescent center on the shore of Lac Edward. During his recovery he began to experience mysterious encounters with strangers. One day he met a "mystical lumberjack." On another he received a small package with a candle made of beeswax from a woman mystic in Germany who was living a life totally devoted to the love of God.

With these incidents there came a sense of "co-vibrations," a communication of a shared atmosphere and feelings from which a vision, a horizon of the new church, began to take shape for Father Oshida.[19]

Weeds and Seeds of Community

Oshida returned to Japan in 1962 and was engaged in parish work in the Tokyo area for six months.[20] During the first year

---

[18] "Evangelization and Inculturation," *Monastic Interreligious Dialogue Bulletin*, 4.

[19] Chisato Kitagawa's translation of Oshida, *Tooi Manazashi*, 98–99, mailed to Lucien Miller on May 19, 2015. Father Watanabe's interview with Chisato Kitagawa on April, 20, 2015, is another source for Oshida's sense of "co-vibrations."

[20] David G. Hackett, *The Silent Dialogue: Zen Letters to a Trappist Abbot* (New York: Continuum, 1996), 53.

of his return, however, he came down with tuberculosis once again and was admitted to St. Mary's International Hospital. Later he was transferred to Sakuramachi Hospital in Musashi Koganei about twenty miles outside Tokyo where he had an operation on his bronchial tubes and also had part of his right lung removed. For his recovery, he was sent to Koike Hospital, a sanitarium in the vicinity of the village of Takamori in Fujimi township, Nagano Prefecture.[21] It was there, in the mountains above Takamori village, that he would establish the Takamori hermitage in 1964.

Speaking to an International Mission Congress, he said it was during his stay at the Koike Hospital sanitarium that "a little community was formed in the rhythm of daily life."[22] A new way of life began, another *madoi* of the sick, the offspring, as it were, of the *madoi* of convalescents at Sendai and Miyagi. Like the previous two, it was not meant to last, even though the participants longed that it would. Over time the patients Oshida met and came to know at Koike Hospital began to speak to him of a "communitarian life."[23] These companions in suffering wanted to join him in a search for a new way of life.[24]

At first he did not know what to say. He had seen experimental communities fail. He felt that trying to bring together persons with dependencies could only lead to catastrophe, for he understood the insecurity of those who lived with the uncertainty of not knowing when their disease might return. At the same time, he sensed that in their hunger for affection, these handicapped and afflicted were chasing a utopian dream world of fraternal love and companionship. In their starry-eyed vision

---

[21] "Evangelization and Inculturation," *Monastic Interreligious Dialogue Bulletin*, 4.

[22] Shigeto Oshida, "Zenna," article for the International Mission Congress, Manila, Philippines, December 2–6, 1979.

[23] Oshida, "Good News from Sinanosakai."

[24] Swami Amaldas, "The Breath of God—To the Zen Center of Soan, Japan," trans. Sarah Schwartzberg, *Monastic Interreligious Dialogue Bulletin* 10 (February 1981).

there lurked the danger of ignoring the simple truth that human beings are imperfect. He was convinced that a community of sick and needy individuals who idealized togetherness and amity would do nothing but deform people. A community formed from such persons would not be viable.

> My answer to their wish was very hard. They had to give themselves away completely and live like a religious, working with their own hands and harvesting their own food. They must live a family life, the normal way for humans, and plant their roots deep within society. Such a way of life is more real than trying to make communities.[25]

Following his discharge from Koganei hospital at Fujimi, he recuperated at the Fujimi sanitarium. Afterwards, he lived an ascetic life of poverty for roughly a year, all alone, like a hermit, staying at two places in a village adjacent to the small city of Fujimi. Intermittently, he inhabited an abandoned temple—actually, little more than a small hut—at Takamori dedicated to Kannon, "Goddess of Mercy," for which he did not have to pay rent.

Some local people said the Kannon temple was haunted, though, and began to wonder about him. They called him "the priest of the chapel," but were surprised that a Christian priest did not construct a church or begin a kindergarten. Gradually their doubts evaporated, and they came to regard him as a person who wished them well, someone who did not have a hidden agenda and was not looking out for his own interests. They were impressed by his genuine dedicated spirit and the fact that he was able to survive, residing alone as he did in that eerie Kannon temple.

He told a village official whom he met that he was interested in something quite simple. "I want to start a *madoi* of God in this area where poor people can live together."[26]

---

[25] Oshida, "Good News from Sinanosakai."
[26] Chisato Kitagawa, *Tooi Manazashi*, 105–6.

By a kind of spiritual osmosis, things developed. Given Oshida's singular charisma, students and other individuals began to gather at the Kannon temple. Gradually Oshida felt comfortable to have people congregating around him there and felt accepted and at home in his surroundings.

As he described those early years during which Takamori Soan was evolving, "we were just running away from our egos with our hands stuck in our pockets and a whistle on our lips."[27] During this period of time, he did not have a clear vision of living an eremitical life, nor did he have any thought of establishing a community at Takamori. He had no project in mind, no idea to develop; he simply lived, facing each moment and each person that came along, trying to respond to whatever need presented itself.

"I had a nostalgia for the Baby Jesus in the manger and was carrying some vision about Jesus," he later wrote. But there was no deliberate thought of, "let us make a community," or "let us start a new religious life."[28] His one certainty was that the ego must disappear so that "the Hand of God" could be at work.[29]

Still, despite this complete absence of any plan, it seems clear to me that Father Oshida had found his niche at the Kannon temple. He was being called to a new life's work, a vocation within the priestly vocation that had been recognized by his spiritual mentors, Father Heuvers and Father Tarte. He was floating on a wave of grace, holding a life preserver that had been thrown to him by One who was bidding him to go with the current and swim in a new direction. He gradually intuited that he had to receive this gift of the Holy Spirit with open arms. What was evolving around him in the Japanese

---

[27] Sasaki, "Encounter with Takamori."

[28] Katrin Åmell, "The Dominican Vincent Oshida Shigeto—A Buddhist Who Has Encountered Christ," *La vie spirituelle*, 731 (1999): 355–68.

[29] Sasaki, "Encounter with Takamori."

Alps was the community of Takamori Soan, with himself as its humble master.

At this point it might be good to add a background note for clarification. Since entering the Order of Preachers in 1951, except for occasional conversations with his provincial, Father Oshida had been relatively silent over the course of thirteen years about what he felt was his deepest vocation. His inner conviction was that obedience means obeying God's Voice,[30] and he determined he must submit to that Voice.

Speaking of his own calling, Thomas Merton wrote: "It has never been practical to leave all things and follow Christ. But it is supernaturally prudent."[31] For Oshida, his "Yes!" was neither practical nor well advised, but an inescapable necessity.

One day, he resolved it was time to return to Tokyo to talk with his religious superior in Japan, Father Bernard M. Trahan, who was the Japanese regional prior of the Canadian Province of the Dominicans. He was pastor at Sukegawa Catholic Church, Fukushima Prefecture, where Oshida had served as a curate for six months. Father Oshida wanted to request permission to leave the conventual community life of the Dominicans and live outside the monastery, finding his way alone.

This encounter took place at some time in 1963 or early 1964. Oshida suspected that his superior had some inkling of his intention even before they talked. He also sensed that Father Trahan was a priest who knew his role was to help his brethren follow the Voice of the Father speaking through his Son.

Oshida spoke directly to Father Trahan: "I shall leave to begin to be myself, to respond to my vocation even as a member of this order." The prior responded, disclosing first his reaction to Oshida's way of doing pastoral ministry when he

---

[30] In Hebrew, *bat kol*, which literally means "daughter of a voice." It refers to a heavenly voice that proclaims God's will or a divine judgment in a matter of legal dispute. The characteristic attributes of the Voice of God are the invisibility of the speaker and the phenomenal quality of its sound.

[31] Quoted in Thomas Merton, "In the Wilderness," *The Merton Seasonal* 40, no. 2 (Summer 2015): 5.

was with him at the Catholic church at Sukegawa, and next his decision: "Father, I do not understand what you do. You sit long hours of *zazen*. That's it. I don't get it. No, not just that. I do not like it. And all the young people are imitating you, sitting." There was a long silence, and then Father Trahan elaborated: "But Father, even if I do not understand it, and however much I might dislike you, I have no right to prevent you from doing so. Please, Father, go ahead with your plan freely."[32]

Oshida told Father Trahan that what he had said was infinitely more precious than any word to indicate that he understood what Oshida wanted and needed to do. He left the superior's room with a *Deo gratias!* ("Thanks be to God") and a *Tibi gratias!* ("Thank you") on his lips. He was overwhelmed by the deep sense that he had experienced the *chikaryū* (地下流), the "subterranean stream," the current of faith flowing from the Unborn Sphere deeply beneath the world's religions, traditions, and indigenous communities in the East and West, forming many different and distinct tributaries.[33]

Father Oshida's reference to the underground river is familiar to all who have known him. It lay deep within his spirit and consciousness and was palpable in his being, his teaching, and the Takamori community. In homilies and retreats he awoke listeners to what he called "Word-Events" in Sacred Scripture. These "Word-Events" emanate from encounters with the sacred river (see chapter 4, "*Sesshin* Part One"). For example, the water Moses saw flowing from the "rock" (Exod 17:6; Num 20:11) is a "Word-Event" that gushes from the "Unborn Sphere."

---

[32] Oshida, "Evangelization and Inculturation."

[33] Rev. Chiemi Ishii Sasaki, "The Idea/Image of Water That Runs Under the Ground—'Faith' for Shigeto Oshida," 2013 Sophia University Summer Theology Workshop, trans. Chisato Kitagawa. Email to Lucien Miller, August 30, 2014. "Unborn Sphere" is Father Oshida's preferred term for Ultimate Reality, the Absolute, the Source, which he often called "the Hand of God." The "subterranean stream" and the "Unborn Sphere" are central symbols in Oshida's portrait of faith, as explained in chapters 2, 3, and 5.

Like the fire at Oshida's celebration of the Eucharist, which we will encounter in chapter 2, biblical water is no ordinary metaphor, but a divine living stream in which Jesus stands at his baptism and sees the heavens open and "the Spirit of God descending like a dove." There he hears a voice declaring "You are my beloved Son; with you I am well pleased" (Matt 3:16-17; Mark 1:9-11).

This same water from the subterranean current is the water Jesus changes into wine at the marriage feast at Cana, revealing his glory, and upon witnessing this, "his disciples began to believe in him" (John 2:2-10). It is the salvific water that is a necessity for us as he tells Nicodemus, the teacher of Israel who comes to him by night: "Very truly, I tell you, no one can enter the kingdom of God without being born of water and Spirit" (John 3:5). Drinking the water Jesus gives, the Samaritan woman at the well "will never be thirsty" (John 4:13-14). At the fall harvest festival, the Jewish Feast of Tabernacles (*Sukkot*), Jesus cries out, promising the coming of the Holy Spirit, "Everyone who drinks of this water will be thirsty again, but those who drink of the water that I will give them will never be thirsty. The water that I will give will become in them a spring of water gushing up to eternal life" (John 4:13-14).[34] Through the water of baptism, one dies and is reborn, is enlightened, and becomes a creature of light.

Having been given permission to leave the conventual life with its Western European form of Christianity to pursue his vocation in his own way, Father Oshida followed his deep longing for poverty and simplicity while remaining a Dominican priest. He wanted simply to be Japanese, "a human being with a nude face," one who had encountered Jesus, a pilgrim priest who believed in Christ.

---

[34] For further references to this divine water, see John 19:34-35 (water and blood flowing from Jesus' side); 1 John 5:6-8 (Jesus came through water and blood); Rev 7:17 (the Lamb will guide his flock to springs of living water); Rev 21:6; 22:1; 22:17 (the gift of life-giving water).

"My heart was weeping," said Oshida of his leave-taking.[35]

To this bittersweet moment of parting with gratitude and tears, with risk and uncertainty, we might append Merton's words on the singularity of a solitary, which aptly fit Shigeto Oshida at this turning point in his life:

> The hermit remains in the world as an unheeded prophet, as a voice crying in the wilderness and as a sign of contradiction . . .

> But . . . even those who fear the solitary nevertheless become fascinated by him, because his very uselessness continues to proclaim that he might after all have some incomprehensible function.[36]

Takamori Soan—Hermitage and International Community

Father Oshida lived the solitary life in the Kannon temple for close to a year. He was then drawn by the Voice and community seekers to settle down at Takamori Soan. As he once

---

[35] Oshida, "Evangelization and Inculturation." Pope Urban II (1042–1099) and St. Thomas Aquinas (1225–1274) would understand both Oshida and his superior. The pope wrote famously that there are "two laws" (*duae leges*) governing religious vocations: the public (a priest must not move between dioceses without the bishop's recommendation) and the private (written in the heart by the Holy Spirit). St. Thomas, a Dominican, quotes Urban's text: "If one . . . driven by the Spirit . . . is guided by the private law, there is no reason why he should be bound by the public law. The private law is, after all, superior to the public law. . . . And who can resist the Holy Spirit? If that Spirit guides a man, then, he should go freely, by virtue of our authority, and even defy the opposition of his bishop. In fact, there is no law for the righteous man—where the Spirit of the Lord is, there is freedom. And if the Spirit guides you, you are no longer subject to the law." See Yves Congar, *I Believe in the Holy Spirit*, vol. 1 (New York: Seabury, 1983), 110–11. The Rule of St. Benedict, chap. 1, states that for some monks, the cenobitic life may be preparatory to the hermit life, arming an anchorite or hermit for "the solitary combat of the desert."

[36] "In the Wilderness," 7

remarked, laconically, "The more I want to be a hermit, the more the people have gathered around me."[37]

One December day in 1964 he received a message saying that ideal land had been found in the Fujimi area. He visited the property and instantly fell in love with its mountainous surroundings and agricultural setting. What immediately drew him was the little spring (小泉 *koizumi*) that emerged in three rivulets from rocks near a rice paddy. For Oshida, it was a sacred place. Koizumi provided drinking water and irrigation to many of the area homes and farms and would become the site of baptisms and prayer at Takamori.

Chisato Kitagawa told me that Koizumi was the reason Father Oshida longed to buy the property. But no one living in this revered rural region ever thought of selling to an outsider. Nor did Father Oshida have the money. He appealed to a town official to facilitate a sale, emphasizing the land would be used for a worthy purpose.

Then he put his trust in God.

Somehow, through the combined generosity of town authorities and local farmers and families, a continuous area of open space and farmland was acquired, and Takamori Soan came into being.

Beginning in 1964, for the next thirty-nine years until his death in 2003, Father Oshida guided the hermitage community in living a contemplative life of poverty and simplicity, self-emptying service to the neighbor and the down and out, and welcoming the stranger belonging to any faith, or none. Gradually, visitors and guests came from around the world, attracted by Takamori Soan's radical openness and its attentiveness to the Voice of God. The president of the Shinto temples of Suwa District rejoiced when he saw a cross being raised, for he felt the land on the border of his jurisdiction was being consecrated and no one living in the venerable region would now have to worry about developers building chalets.

---

[37] Oshida, "Evangelization and Inculturation."

Oshida admitted that it was very possible that none of the local people knew that every morning Mass was being celebrated in the new chapel with a thatched roof, but he was sure they sensed that the land was being used in such a way as to give them hope. He insisted that the property belonged only to God and the poor, the ill, and the suffering, "to those who make their life a total offering." Takamori Soan was to be run by the poor and supported by whatever they could offer; it would be a site of and for the spiritually poor.

> This is a place where the weak and the poor produce by their hands the food they need, in a style of religious life. It is a place where the weak are healed of their great disease, which is dependency . . . A place where anyone can contemplate without concern for his ideology or his religion.[38]

The way of poverty and self-emptiness the Takamori community was following was full of grace; surprise followed surprise at every turn. To Oshida what unfolded was inexplicable, except as an intimation of the gospel of Jesus: "Very truly, I tell you, unless a grain of wheat falls into the earth and dies, it remains just a single grain; but if it dies, it bears much fruit" (John 12:24).

In Father Oshida's words: "Some grains of wheat fell to earth. . . ."

Captivated by what had transpired through the unfolding of Takamori in the early 1960s, Father Oshida was surely mindful of the fire he lit at the daily celebration of Eucharist when he said, "This fire will pass from heart to heart."

Strictly speaking, according to Catholic Church requirements, the Dominican Order should have asked permission from the local bishop for Father Oshida to move from his assigned parish at Sukegawa Church to Takamori. That would have been the bishop of the Diocese of Yokohama, Lucas

---

[38] Oshida, "Good News from Sinanosakai."

Katsusaburo Arai (荒井勝三郎), whose jurisdiction included Nagano Prefecture where Takamori Soan is located. It was rumored Bishop Arai was displeased that he was not consulted about the agreement between the Dominican prior and Father Oshida.

Be that as it may, the bishop came to accept and welcome the change. When Father Oshida took a temporary position filling in for the pastor at Sukegawa Church, Bishop Arai said to him, "Please make sure to return to Takamori Soan."[39]

Some twenty-five years later, in 1990, Father Oshida organized and hosted the 1990 Asian Bishops' Conference at Takamori.[40] The convocation may well be viewed as a singular affirmation of his way of living out his Dominican vocation, of heeding Jesus' call to freedom, the inner law written in the heart by the Holy Spirit. When Father Oshida looked inward, he must also have sensed that the fact that the Asian Bishops Conference was willing to meet at Takamori was a validation of the vow he made at his ordination in 1961: "I shall not lie any more to myself and to You."

---

[39] Chisato Kitagawa, interview with Father Hiroshige Watanabe, OP, at Takamori Soan, April 20, 2015.

[40] Verboven, "Vincent Shigeto Oshida (Japan)," 189.

CHAPTER TWO

Hermit and Pilgrim

A few days after attending Father William Johnston's Charismatic-Zen *sesshin* in 1976, I left for Japan. Following my interior assent to his urgent bidding, I simply had to visit Father Oshida and his Takamori Hermitage in the Japanese Alps. As I said earlier, I "jumped ship" at the Tokyo Airport, lying to the Japanese authorities that I would stay overnight at the Tokyo YMCA and catch my family's connecting flight to San Francisco in the morning. Without any knowledge of Japanese save for courtesy phrases, let alone a Japanese visa, I somehow found my way to the huge Tokyo train station and wandered about until kind people guided me to the train for Nagano northwest of Tokyo, situated in the "Japanese Alps," and thence to Takamori Station. I called Takamori Soan and was surprised to hear the welcoming voice of a Western woman who gave me directions speaking colloquial English. A short taxi ride winding up through villages and mountainsides took me to Father Shigeto Oshida's community.

With my first glimpse of Takamori,[1] I felt I had dropped from the sky into a Japanese paradise: a handful of small cottages amid the woods built in traditional Japanese farmhouse

[1] For an insightful overview of daily life at Takamori Soan and a personal exploration of Christian and Buddhist similarities and differences, see David Hackett, *The Silent Dialogue: Zen Letters to a Trappist Abbot* (New York: Continuum, 1996), esp. chap. 5.

Takamori entrance

style with thatched roofs, an adjacent rice field of golden stalks rustling in the breeze, and a crystal creek bubbling nearby—everywhere and everything imbued with an atmosphere of silence, poverty, harmony, and aesthetic beauty.

After a welcoming and tea with Sister Maria Kawasumi, the principal lifelong assistant to Father Oshida and attendant at Takamori, l was free to wander about. The main building was a gathering point for community meals, cooking, and clothes washing. Built by the community members out of used materials, it had a Japanese-style tile roof, walls and verandas made from old wood, and a distinctive rustic look, simple and charming to the eye.

The dining area had a low *kotatsu*-style dining table with space underneath it for stretching one's legs and, in cool weather, a charcoal stove for keeping feet and legs comfortably warm during meals. The absence of modern conveniences—television, air-conditioning, electrical appliances, a flush toilet—

Takamori main building

epitomized for me a lifestyle of simplicity and poverty of spirit. My hands, being empty, were free to receive, and the scales of greed and self fell from my eyes—at least temporarily.

Adjacent to the main building was a *kotoba* or memorial, an open shed with a narrow thatched roof and wooden strips of calligraphy hanging beneath, commemorating benefactors and others significantly related to Takamori Soan.

At the edge of the vegetable garden was a rough weathered garden hut embodying the *wabi-sabi* mode of beauty—utter poverty, imperfection, artful mending, simplicity, imperma-nence, refinement, and melancholy. A plain guesthouse had bedcovers and thick, quilted cushions for sleeping on the floor.

Nearby, in the woods or next to a building—I cannot re-member which—I encountered a semi-hidden sign "*Sesshin*," (Japanese 接心; Chinese *Shè xīn* 攝心), literally "touch the heart-mind," encouraging intensive *zazen*. It could be roughly trans-lated as, "Conserve Heart-Mind," "Nurture Heart-Mind,"

Omidō

"Concentrate Heart-Mind," or "Unite in One Person Heart-Mind." The sign struck me as a gesture or instruction—a reminder to residents or visitors why they are at Takamori—to meditate or pray with their whole being, with their mind and heart, as one. Mind and Heart—"the engine of self," as Patricia Hampl, the master of writing memoirs, calls it,[2] or perhaps, in Buddhist terms, the engine of "no-self."

Hidden amid deciduous trees and shrubbery was a small, exquisite building, the "*Omidō*," 御聖堂, or chapel, with a handmade multilayered straw roof and traditional windows latticed with horizontal strings of wood and bamboo. "*Omidō*," as community members affectionately refer to it when speaking English, rather than "the *Omidō*," was the very first structure built at Takamori by community members. In her lyrical essay, "Encounter with Takamori—Encounter with the Deep Stream,"

---

[2] Patricia Hampl, *The Florist's Daughter* (Orlando: Harcourt, 2007), 110.

the Protestant Pastor Reverend Chiemi Ishii Sasaki describes the chapel as being akin to a Japanese tea cottage, "with its bottomless silence, pure light and merciful whispers, [it] is the center of Takamori Hermitage."[3]

Everything in it was in harmony with a beauty shining from an inner light—the reed window, the black luster of the walls from countless fires set in an iron pot during the celebration of the Eucharist, the carpet woven from straw, the altar on the floor made from a single wooden plank, the altar cloth woven by a Takamori sister, the kiln fired pottery chalice, and, affixed vertically to the chapel wall, the tabernacle made from a hollowed-out log with a pine door and small pine box inside to house the Blessed Sacrament.

When Professor Chisato Kitagawa visited the *Omidō*, he was awestruck. "Unexpectedly, the room was filled with the Holy Spirit. Its presence was tangible."[4]

Behind the chapel was the Remembrance Wood dedicated to those victims who were killed by the Japanese military during World War II and in preceding eras: the Holy Innocents who suffer through no fault of their own. It was made up of a number of memorial logs and poles raised vertically by the community members of Takamori Soan.

Rev. Sasaki elaborates:

> One log stands for every war's victims. The Pacific war's victims, the victims of the Japanese occupation of Korea, the victims of the Sino-Japanese War, especially the Nanjing Massacre in China,[5] the victims of the Philippines and Pacific islands wars. Here is a mourning prayer for all those

---

[3] Rev. Chiemi Ishii Sasaki, "Encounter with Takamori—Encounter with the Deep Stream," unpublished manuscript.

[4] Chisato Kitagawa email, June 5, 2015.

[5] For six weeks Japanese soldiers killed, tortured, raped, and pillaged many thousands of Chinese civilians, men, women, and children, as well as non-combatant military. Oshida was overwhelmed hearing the news. Father Hiroshige Watanabe, OP, Kitagawa email, June 5, 2015.

victims forgotten by the hidden Japanese conscience in the silence of the statesmen.[6]

Father Oshida's short poem and calligraphy written in his hand were inscribed on the central tree trunk:

限りなき

なみだの海に

消えず 立たなむ

茂人

Kagiri naki

namida no umi ni

kiezu tatanamu

We shall stand

without disappearing

in the sea of infinite tears

Shigeto

One day infinite tears were shed by Father Oshida and a woman visitor from the Philippines. She had been sent by her spiritual director to see him because she could not forgive Japan and the Japanese for atrocities she had witnessed in her country during the Second Word War. Once as she was standing in a jungle clearing with a group of her neighbors, a Japanese soldier tore a baby girl from her mother's arms, threw her into the air, and bayoneted the infant as she fell before her mother's horrified eyes. Saying little, Father led the woman around the Remembrance Wood, stopping by each tree that

---

[6] Sasaki, "Encounter with Takamori."

was a sorrowful memorial dedicated to victims of each Japanese war. When they reached Father Oshida's tree, he slowly chanted aloud his English translation of his poem. After a long silence they both wept.

"I think I may have reached forgiveness" cried the woman.[7]

One day Sister Kawasumi, responding to my request, whispered in my ear at dinner hour, "You can visit Father Oshida now." Apparently, she was tasked with protecting him from too many visitors knocking at his door.

When I entered his living quarters, a poor hut hidden in the surrounding woods, I felt the glow of *wabi-sabi*, the aesthetic of beauty in traditional Japanese culture. Everything spoke of imperfection, impermanence, austerity, and the intimacy of natural objects: rough walls made of unfinished planks, papers piled on a desk, books here and there in no particular order. As I looked forward through a series of doorless small spaces, I saw Father Oshida sitting behind his desk as he was leafing through a beautiful Japanese manuscript that looked like it was handwritten in classical Japanese calligraphy.

Gazing up and seeing me, as if from afar, he watched me with a notable look of bemused serenity as I awkwardly made my way forward, my big body bumping against a chair or two, and entered his room through a narrow passageway. He had a kind look, though rather drawn, as though he were somewhat worn down by being a hermit in community, a host with

---

[7] It was a blessing to hear Father Oshida share this story. As I note in the final chapter where I describe a "Blessings Day" that took place in 2015 to consecrate a memorial dedicated to Father Oshida, the poem points beyond Japan's sorrow to our own guilt and forgetfulness as Americans, calling us to remember and pray for the Holy Innocents we have destroyed in the enslavement of Black Americans, the genocide of Native Americans, abortion, and civilians killed by saturation bombings in Germany, Japan, Vietnam, and Cambodia, and by drone attacks in Afghanistan. We are called to stand fast in solidarity with guiltless victims—to confess our guilt and mourn their loss, to resist war and iniquity, to feed the hungry and shelter the poor, and to never give up remembering the Holy Innocents, "lest we forget" and repeat our evil acts of maiming and destroying.

Oshida in his cottage

too many visitors and their concerns. With a bit of a giggle, he rose and came forward smiling graciously, and opened his arms wide in greeting. Gesturing to two hard, stuffed pillows before his desk, he invited me to sit down. I noticed he was holding a note I had written to him before leaving Taiwan, asking if I could visit Takamori.

"So, what brings you to Takamori?" he asked warmly, seemingly more than just curious about this rather large, tall American visitor who had to stoop low and tread carefully to find his way through his home. After we sat down cross-legged on our pillows he quoted a sentence by Father William Johnston I had cited in my note: "I believe that God is the mystery of mysteries and that when we meet God we can only say that we experience Nothing or Emptiness."

"Do you agree?" he asked.

I was ready for him. I pulled out a page of Johnston quotations from my Nepalese shoulder bag I had bought years back in Hong Kong and responded with another Johnston insight: "We used to say that dialogue between the religions is necessary for world peace. Now we can say that dialogue between the religions is necessary for world survival."

"I don't really understand that first citation in my letter to you," I explained. "Though I'd like to, especially since," I bragged, "I just completed a Christian-Zen charismatic retreat with Father Johnston and trust you can interpret the quote for me."

"Actually," I went on, after a nervous silent pause in which he said nothing, "I certainly agree with most everything Father Johnston says, even if I don't always understand. But I sure do want to ask you what you think about dialogue between religions."

Father Oshida winced, a look of kind disdain on his face.

"Too many questions," he declared. "Intellectual, not spiritual."

Chagrinned, I was completely undone. I had prepared for this exact moment so carefully. And now—too many questions, when I had hardly begun.

He briefly asked me instead about my family, my being a professor, and a little about our family life together in Taiwan. Absolutely nothing about my faith, my Catholicism, my Christian-Zen experience.

Then, he got up, sat behind his desk, and politely waved goodbye.

Daily morning Eucharist during the week I stayed at Takamori was like nothing I had experienced before. I entered the darkness and silence of the chapel with a deep bow, my palms placed together in the traditional Buddhist *gasshō* style. Father Oshida sat utterly still, a single candle on an upright log next to him. For a vestment, he wrapped himself in a beige-white garment that covered his head and hands. Each day there were usually a dozen or so staff and Japanese and foreign guests sitting cross-legged on cushions meditating, with one or two on their knees or sitting on a simple stool.

Father was always keen to have the altar prepared just so, with a deep reverence for "the logos of a table" [8]—a wooden board on the floor, three white altar linens and chalice exactly laid in place. For the washing of hands there was a bowl of pure Koizumi water with white gravel gleaming in the bottom. Beside the altar was a large, venerable-looking clay pot sitting on a block of wood.

Seeing this setting, I felt Father Oshida's enormous respect for tradition and the dignity of the moment, for what was taking place before our eyes and within and for each person. Everyone seemed completely present and aware of the miracle unfolding before us. As for Father Oshida, he was for me, in Merton's terms, "one whose mind and heart are integrated and illuminated by grace," the *holokleros* in Orthodox spirituality, the one St. Paul prays that we all become. [9]

---

[8] "The *logos* of a table: realized in the mystical table which is the altar around which the brethren gather for the fraternal meal at which the Risen Christ will be mystically present and will break bread." Thomas Merton, "Lecture Notes on Theology and Mysticism," in *Merton and Hesychasm: The Prayer of the Heart; The Eastern Church,* ed. Bernadette Dieker and Jonathan Montaldo (Louisville, KY: Fons Vitae, 2003), 441. The *logos* of a table belongs to the *logoi* of things and beings, part of the divine economy, God's plan for and within things, the inner meaning or essence of things, the mysterious norms hidden in things by the Creator, the hidden wisdom of God in things. Oshida's wood plank altar and the experience of his Mass is resplendent with echoes of Eastern Orthodoxy's hesychastic tradition of contemplative prayer. See David Bradshaw, "The *Logoi* of Beings in Greek Patristic Thought," in *Toward an Ecology of Transfiguration: Orthodox Christian Perspectives on Environment, Nature, and Creation,* ed. John Chryssavgis and Bruce V. Foltz (New York: Fordham University Press, 2013), 9–13; Basil Pennington, "Thomas Merton and Byzantine Spirituality," in *Merton and Hesychasm,* 153–68.

[9] Merton, "Lecture Notes on Theology and Mysticism," 439. St. Paul, "May the God of peace himself sanctify you entirely, and may your spirit and soul and body be kept sound and blameless at the coming of our Lord Jesus Christ" (1 Thess 5:23).

Omidō chapel interior

We began Mass in profound silence and breathing deeply—
a silence and breath that imbued the entire Eucharist.[10]
Rev. Sasaki hauntingly describes the unfolding of the chapel
liturgy:

> As we sit in *zazen*, we become engulfed by the silence of
> the *Omidō*. It penetrates our bodies, becoming clear and
> transparent, hypnotic and tangible, as time passes. Chant-
> ing psalms, we breathe in and out, long and deeply, coor-
> dinating our breath together in the breath we share. "I"
> disappears, words are born anew, only to vanish. The breath

[10] The Mass, also referred to as the Eucharist, is the central liturgical ritual
in the Catholic Church. In it the Word of God is proclaimed, prayers are offered, and bread and wine become the sacrament of the Body and Blood of
Jesus the Christ. The term "mass" comes from the dismissal at the conclusion
of the Latin Roman Rite: "*Ite, missa est.*" In Christian usage, "dismissal" sug-
gests "mission" as well, i.e., "Go and do your mission as a follower of Christ."

of all beings, their groaning and pain, become a soundless
Voice, coming into being and disappearing. Father Oshida
says, "To pray is to ride on breath." Such a prayer is what
exists here in the *Omidō*, the prayer of Takamori Soan.[11]

The "Voice" Rev. Sasaki cites is a key sacred word Father
Oshida used constantly throughout his teaching, writing, and
speaking engagements, referring to a concept that we shall
often encounter in subsequent chapters. It is the Hebrew *Bat
Kol*, revelation through sound, a heavenly or divine voice announcing divine reactions to certain events, proclaiming God's
will or judgment.

As noted in chapter 1, for Father Oshida obedience meant
obeying the *Bat Kol*, the Voice of God.

"Coming into being and disappearing" is a mystical koan
or word-puzzle that to my mind invokes death and resurrection. It echoes the several descriptions of the disciples' experience of the risen Christ. At the breakfast barbecue, for example,
where he cooks fish and bread at the Sea of Tiberias for his
disciples (John 21:1-14), he is visible, in the flesh, then disappears. Christ disappears in his death upon the cross, then appears again in a conversation with followers on the road to
Emmaus and the silent meal they share (Luke 24:13-35), in an
encounter with Mary Magdalene at the empty tomb (John
20:14-18), and in an appearance to "doubting Thomas" and
the disciples in the locked Upper Room, only to disappear
again.

Analogously, in Father Oshida's Mass at Takamori's *Omidō*,
worshipers disappear in the silence, breath, chant, and word,
then reappear in the moans and pains of Creation, only to
disappear again in a silent Voice.

Following the reading of the gospel, moved by Word and
Spirit, Father Oshida would turn to some event or person deep

---

[11] Sasaki, "Encounter with Takamori." The translation is by Chisato
Kitagawa in an email to Lucien Miller, March 17, 2017.

in his consciousness. His speech and demeanor were softly dramatic, akin perhaps to a Kabuki actor. He might be gentle and tender, pointed and angry, or chortling ecstatically, but always stunning. He spoke in Japanese, then in English, and sometimes in French, depending on the guests. As he preached there were tears and laughter, both his and ours. Usually some deep awareness touched him—the arms race, the threat of atomic annihilation, the mystical experience of a woman visitor who is a Japanese Buddhist monk, the loving self-giving of a Takamori community sister or groundskeeper, or the threat peasant rice farmers around Takamori village and Takamori Hermitage were facing from polluters, developers, or the government.

One morning at the prayer of the faithful following his homily, he prayed for the handicapped, captives, and martyrs outside the visible church, and for mercy.

"Forgiveness is unity," he declared.

At the beginning of the offertory, Father Oshida did something utterly new to me in the Mass. He lit a fire made from twigs and paper set in the clay pot beside the altar, returned to his cushion and began to sing softly. As the flames crackled and the smoke rose through an opening in the upmost part of the chapel roof, fine ashes settled about the chapel and on each worshiper.

After the consecration, Father Oshida asked that this Body and Blood give us courage and simplicity. "Let God take us in his strength to the abyss," he prayed. The snapping of fire, the snowfall of ashes, and the faint fragrance of smoke and incense joined in a shared moment of sacred presence as we handed Christ's Body and Blood from person to person. The Mass was a mystical transformation for all of us. For a brief moment we lived and breathed, as it were, cup and plate, breath and chant, tabernacle and altar, even Father Oshida's vestments and downcast eyes. We were outside of time, beyond self, consumed in the body and blood and the fire.

A still, quiet ecstasy.

Fire-Mass

My tentative, hesitant, Catholic self became unmoored with the rising flames and falling ashes, discovering if not my true self then my truer self, riding the breath of all being, coming into being, and disappearing in the soundless Voice, suspended in the prayer of Takamori.

The significance of fire in the Mass should have been obvious to me but was not.

In *Confession of a Fisherman* (*Ryooshi no Kokuhaku*), Father Oshida's Japanese translation of the Gospel of John, he asks:

Why does fire attract us? When wood goes through transformation and becomes fire, we feel some sure presence
behind the flame that may burn out soon. That sure presence . . . comes to us with certainty. On this fire we cook
and we eat and exchange our presence. It was in that friendship circle and gathering (*madoi*) that human beings started
burning offerings to God and offered their food cooked on
the fire. The sense of that sure presence that people felt
through history was shared by the fishermen at the sea of
Galilee. That sure presence is with us now being all the
substance of the material world that surrounds us.[12]

It was not until years later that I remembered the obvious
connection between God and fire in the Hebrew Bible. Speaking to Moses, the LORD says, "Has any people ever heard the
voice of a god speaking out of a fire, as you have heard, and
lived? " (Deut 4:33).

In the New Testament, John the Baptist referring to Jesus,
says, "I baptize you with water for repentance, but one who
is more powerful than I is coming after me; I am not worthy
to carry his sandals. He will baptize you with the Holy Spirit
and fire" (Matt 3:11). The association of baptism with fire is
clear. But a believer like me who has experienced that "sure
presence" at Father Oshida's Eucharist can only wish fire were
part of the liturgy of every Mass—an indoor fire hazard and
therefore surely impossible—lending visible credence to
Catholic doctrine, which teaches that it is the Holy Spirit who

---

[12] *Confession of a Fisherman* (*Ryooshi no Kokuhaku*), English translation by
Chisato Kitagawa. Oshida refers to the story of the breakfast barbecue at the
beach around which the disciples gathered with the risen Christ in the Gospel of John 21:1-19. The union of fire, the Holy Spirit, and the Eucharist is an
ancient Christian teaching, most noted annually in the Easter fire that begins
the liturgy of the Easter Vigil on Holy Saturday, representing Christ's resurrection. See Yves Congar, *I Believe in the Holy Spirit*; for Holy Spirit and fire
references in Ephrem of Syria, Isaac of Antioch, and others, see 3:22, 105,
262–66.

transforms the bread and wine into the Body and Blood of Jesus the Christ. The Takamori Mass was an experience of Pentecost, a taste of the Holy Spirit in the form of "tongues, as of fire" that came to rest on the heads of the disciples (Acts 2:3).

Everyone participated in daily chores at Takamori Soan. My job that week was working in the strawberry bed, cultivating and transplanting. Of course, everything had to be done correctly and contemplatively, in Father Oshida's inimitable way. This meant learning through experience, trial and error, but most importantly, observing and listening in silence.

One day several of us went to the Takamori rice paddy to harvest the late August rice. After everyone had a good laugh, enjoying the fact that there were no rubber boots big enough in Japan to fit my size-14 feet, we grabbed scythes and set to work. I thought I was doing a pretty good job cutting the rice stalks close to the ground and stacking them in tepee-like cones, although my tepees kept collapsing.

"No, no, never that way," Oshida shouted at me, "but this way."

He demonstrated "this way," cutting and stacking gracefully and exactly. I grasped the beautiful difference in the way he held the rice stalks and cut, placing them in elegant stacks standing in a perfect row. But I simply couldn't get it right.

"Listen to the rice," Oshida urged. "Be the farmer. The farmer listens. The rice tells him when it wants to be planted, fertilized, weeded, and harvested. How it should be cut and stacked. He doesn't read it out of a book. Listen, listen, listen. The rice will tell you everything."

After a while, I stood back and watched the exquisite scene of the harvest unfolding all around me, experiencing Rev. Sasaki's words describing the laborious yet delicate work of rice farming at 3,300 feet elevation. "There is nothing comparable to the beauty of people working in the same rice field with Father Oshida saying, 'The work must sink deeply into one's body,'" she writes. "We are also cultivated in this effort

. . . because our wrongs and distress fall into nature. Takamori's rice fields have the power to absorb them."[13]

Across from the rice paddies of Takamori Soan is Koizumi, "Little Spring." Koizumi irrigates the Takamori rice fields and its waters flow through the interior of homes of residents throughout the valley.

Koizumi is something mysterious. It springs from the base of a mountain in three small tributaries that immediately form a single stream. Spring, summer, winter, and fall, Koizumi always gushes at the same volume and speed. The emersion point is a place of pilgrimage and baptisms, and for me during my week's stay, it was a favorite place for meditation and peace.

One sunny afternoon during an afternoon break, I followed the spring's course to an elegant traditional Japanese home where I encountered the owner, a woman dressed in a kimono, watering the flowers in her garden. Naive me, I thought she was wearing a formal gown and guessed she was coming from or going to some special occasion or event, but for all I knew, she was wearing the clothing she did every day.

When I pointed to the water flowing through an opening in a wall of her home, she bowed and then waved to me, inviting me in.

She graciously showed me the traditional features of her home—identifying them in Japanese as she pointed them out to me, while I hastily jotted down their names: tatami flooring, *zabuton* (thin pillows for sitting), *shoji* and *fusuma* (latticed windows and sliding panels of wood-framed translucent or opaque paper to let in light and shadows), and *ranma* (an elaborately carved wooden panel that is placed above a sliding door). In one room there was a *tokonoma*, an elevated interior niche displaying a calligraphy scroll and a single flower in a vase. I marveled at the *wagoya* above me, the complex post-and-lintel interior construction made without nails, and I admired the

---

[13] Sasaki, "Encounter with Takamori."

folding screens decorated with paintings, and the *engawa*, the veranda that circled the home, from which were hung last night's quilts and comforters to air. The captivating sight of Koizumi's brook coursing through wooden troughs across the center of one spacious room was enchanting, an aesthetic vision that perfectly complemented all the crafted aesthetic beauty of my hostess's home.

At Takamori Soan, I soon discovered our own community work came second. If a village neighbor or farmer was in need, we responded immediately and stopped whatever we were doing. One afternoon during meditation, a farmer came to Father Oshida and whispered in his ear, interrupting prayer and *zazen*. He nodded and gestured, and suddenly all of us were off and making our way to a neighboring farm. We spent a long hot afternoon loading a truck with heavy bags of rice and great bundles of rice stalks, followed by a delicious farm feast in an old farmhouse with a thatched roof and a tiny entrance door. I let everyone enter ahead of me, as I especially wanted to be polite, and, frankly, was a bit embarrassed about my six-foot two-inch frame that towered over everybody.

How was I going to get into the farmhouse? I literally had to squeeze my body through the door and burst inside, like toothpaste popping from a tube, knocking people this way and that as I crashed forward. The farmhands burst into laughter at my grand entrance, pointing one by one to my giant feet stuffed into undersize rubber boots, cupping their hands over their mouths as they giggled gleefully. It was all in good fun, and everyone welcomed me with joy. But for me, if ever there were a moment to lose face in Japan, this had to be it.

A Hermit's Travels

Given their common contemplative spirits, the contrast between Thomas Merton and Shigeto Oshida is illuminating.

Jonathan Montaldo, Merton scholar, writer, and retreat guide, remarks, "Merton's journey is much more interior and

Oshida reading Japanese paper

'mental,' whereas Shigeto Oshida chooses to love the world in ways Merton only aspired to. Merton could not have founded a Takamori Soan."[14]

Except for rare meetings outside the Abbey of Gethsemani, such as with the Japanese Buddhist scholar, D. T. Suzuki in New York, Merton's travels were largely visionary, through dreams or in his imagination, e.g., his dream of a Black woman who embraced him or his prescient dream of a nurse calling him (she becomes real in his love affair with "M. S.").[15]

Where Merton and Oshida were alike is in their almost gravitational pull to the eremitical life and their attraction to indigenous peoples. Regarding the latter, Merton urges Latin American poets and writers to return to their native indigenous

---

[14] Jonathan Montaldo email, December 5, 2016.
[15] The identity of "M. S." has not been made public.

cultural roots, which are the "hidden springs" of their "sub-conscious heritage."[16] At one point in a 1959 journal entry, he says he needs "something that is beyond my capacity to know," which he calls "a primitive life." He wants to make a journey to "a primitive place" among "primitive people" and die there. He longs to go "to somewhere where I have never been or thought of going"— a pilgrimage, like Abraham's, "going where he knows not where at the call of God."[17]

To me there is an abstract spiritual quality to Merton's sense of travel that transcends a yearning for the primitive. Merton himself describes the journey as "at the same time a going out and a 'return.'"[18] His description echoes the classical Chinese sense of "return," *guei*, 歸, the internal pining to return to where our minds and hearts long to be and where they belong in the first place,[19] something that I referred to in the introduction when describing how I felt mysteriously drawn to Father Oshida before I knew him. When we become aware of the "unity-in-difference" of wholeness,[20] of God and ourselves as one, Christopher Pramuk writes, "it is like coming home to where we have never been before."[21]

---

[16] See Merton's interview with Chilean poet Hernan Lavin Cerda, "Answers for Hernan Lavin Cerda: On War, Technology, and the Intellectual," *The Merton Annual* 2 (1989): 5–12.

[17] Thomas Merton, *A Search for Solitude: Pursuing the Monk's True Life* (San Francisco: HarperSanFrancisco, 1996), 318; "From Pilgrimage to Crusade," in Thomas Merton, *Mystics and Zen Masters* (New York: Farrar, Strauss and Giroux, 1967), 95. Donald Grayston cites these passages in *Thomas Merton and the Noonday Demon: The Camaldoli Correspondence* (Cambridge: Lutterworth Press, 2015), 245–46, reminding us how dearly Merton venerates the Indigenous and their ways of life.

[18] Merton, *Search for Solitude*.

[19] See Lucien Miller, "Poetry as Contemplation: T'ao Ch'ien's 'Homing' (Guei qulai ci, 歸 去 來 辭), and William Wordsworth's 'Tintern Abbey,'" *Journal of the Institute of Chinese Studies* 6, no. 2 (December 1973): 563–84.

[20] Merton's phrase.

[21] Christopher Pramuk, *At Play In Creation* (Collegeville, MN: Liturgical Press, 2015), 90, 99.

As for Father Oshida, his attraction to primitive worlds was concrete and crystal clear.

One day during the weeklong "September Conference," a gathering Father Oshida convened of people from around the world dedicated to living among and serving the poor and resisting nuclear annihilation,[22] he suddenly stopped the proceedings and led all of us participants on a long walk around the hillsides of Takamori to a small local museum of anthropology that housed artifacts and dioramas of primitive Japanese society, a visible representation of the subconscious heritage of Japan. He was ecstatic showing us around, delighting in what he considered the "real" Japan. He found contemporary Indigenous peoples' way of living truly genuine and their elemental heritage an arresting contrast to the spiritual decay of modern society. He spent time living among native tribes in Saipan and the Philippines, partially, as Chisato Kitagawa notes, because they constituted a desired "discourse sphere" for a "real" or authentic person-to-person encounter. He did not trust metaphysical language. His trust was in "event" (*koto*, 事) language—a down-to-earth communication between one actual person and another.[23]

The kind of communication Oshida sought is superbly exemplified in his encounter with Hungarian artist Joseph Domjan (József Domján) that I will describe in chapter 3, and with servants of the poor at his September Conference.

Travel became a decidedly significant part of Father Oshida's vocation and mission, seemingly a rebirth of Takamori abroad, of "running away from our egos with our hands stuck in our pockets and a whistle on our lips." He may well have discovered a new way of wandering freely and of spiritual encounter, following his vocation to live outside a Dominican priory or

---

[22] Oshida considered the conference held September 23–30, 1981, an emergency meeting in the face of a worldwide crisis of faith and the threat of nuclear annihilation. See "September Meeting" in the epilogue.

[23] Chisato Kitagawa personal communication.

House of Studies. Travel was not something he did separately from his role as contemplative leader of the Takamori Hermitage community. It was an outgrowth from it and a further response to listening to the Voice.

This evolution came into full fruition in the years following his attendance at the East-West Monastic Dialogue Conference of Benedictines and Cistercians in Bangkok, Thailand, in 1968, where he met Thomas Merton just before Merton was tragically electrocuted after his morning address to the conference attendees. Perhaps this trip and his encounter with Merton, which coincided with the latter's first and last Asian pilgrimage, awoke Father Oshida to a new dimension of travel in his life's work.

Following the conference and in subsequent years, he made many trips abroad, responding to the invitations he received to give retreats and lectures, responding as well to the Voice that called him to particular people, places, and situations. Among the countries he visited were Thailand, India, Bangladesh, Vietnam, Hong Kong, Taiwan, South Korea, Philippines, Saipan, Poland and other European countries, Lebanon, Israel, Canadian provinces, and states in the United States.[24]

In addition, during his partial participation in the international Interfaith Pilgrimage for Peace and Life (1994–1995) organized by his friend, the Buddhist monk Gyoshu Sasamori Shonin, and the Nipponzan-Myōhōji Buddhist Order, he traversed other countries as well.[25] It was an extraordinary walk from Auschwitz to Hiroshima, marking the fiftieth anniversary of the end of World War II, an estimated ten-thousand mile

---

[24] Sister Maria Kawasumi, interview with Chisato Kitagawa at Takamori Soan, June 5, 2015. Kitagawa email to Lucien Miller, June 5, 2015.

[25] According to Buddhist monk Sasamori Shonin, Father Oshida attended these portions of the peace pilgrimage: December 4–8, 1994, the entirety of the Convocation at Auschwitz; January 29–February 25, portions of the march through Israel and Palestine; February 26–March 8, the entirety of the Iraq march; June 18–August 2, portions of the march through the Philippines. Samamori Shonin email to Chisato Kitagawa, October 15, 2015.

journey through some eighteen countries scarred by old conflicts and the wounds of present-day wars. It was an act of collective remembering, reparation, compassion, and healing, meant for the transformation of self and world.[26]

Father Oshida passed away eight years after that pilgrimage. Given his weakened condition, he must have anticipated that this journey for peace, which he would not complete, could not but make the day of his death more imminent.[27]

His way of being both a hermit in community and world traveler reveals something else, a path and a calling both singular and mysterious. As we have noted, when he left the conventual life he lived for a year or so as a hermit in an abandoned temple, and he would speak occasionally of wanting one day to be a hermit, but his role and obligations at Takamori delayed that actualization; he lived for others.

My own experience of him was as a solitary mystic whose radiance enlightened others and whose communion with others and other locations filled his own being with the holy presence of God. His solitary self blossomed in union with the worldwide mystical communion encountered at Takamori. Like Merton, his life seems contradictory (alternately drawn to solitude and company, self-removal and reaching out, a silent tongue and a conference talk) but he was in fact consistent and of a piece (complementary opposites of hermit and community teacher, solitary and traveler). Always when he

---

[26] Katsu Harada et al., eds., Reports from the "Interfaith Pilgrimage for Peace and Life 1995," *Newsletter Jyunrei* 3, 4, no. 4 (1995), Tokyo: Meiji Gakuin University, http://www.jyunrei.net/jyunrei95e3.htm (accessed November 5, 2022). See also Lisa Roche and Dan Turner, literary eds.; Daniel A. Brown and Skip Schiel, photo eds., *Ashes and Light: Auschwitz to Hiroshima, Interfaith Pilgrimage for Peace and Life 1995* (Leverett, MA: Nipponzan Myohoji, 1996), http://teeksaphoto.org/Archive/Exhibits/95PilgrF/AshesLightF/Ashes LightBook.html (accessed November 5, 2022). For critical analysis, see Peter Sutherland, "Walking Middle Passage History in Reverse: Interfaith Pilgrimage, Virtual Communitas and World-Recathesis," *Etnofoor* 20, no. 1 (2007): 31–62.

[27] Chisato Kitagawa email to Lucien Miller, December 16, 2018.

stayed with us before directing a retreat he would declare: "Don't let anyone know I am here."

But it was not to be. The phone would soon ring and ring again after his arrival, and notes would come in the mail—of course, the word of his travels had somehow gotten out, probably through himself—and he would always respond. Often when he arrived at our home, he seemed in a state of near exhaustion and collapse. Suddenly, hearing the phone or opening a waiting letter, he would break his own orders and run roughshod over our roles as publicity controllers and protectors of temporary enclosure. Somehow he would revive, fully energized, and return to his true self, listening compassionately or laughing uproariously as he responded to a request to visit someone or resolve an issue.

His desire to be a hermit was transformed into a vocation to be a solitary among others, a servant of poverty and simplicity, a spiritual master among fellow pilgrims, following the call of the Voice. In a deep sense, Oshida was always a solitary at heart, whether living alone when he left conventual life, following the way of solitude and silence at Takamori, or traveling.

Father Oshida's travel also tells us something about who he was as a person, and more particularly, as a Japanese person.

> As a person, Father Oshida wanted to be with people. He treasured person-to-person events, as in his encounter with his novice master Father Tarte blowing his bird-whistle, experiencing language as celebration. He yearned to be with the suffering and the poor, personally present where they are, from the depth of their existence and yours, and to listen. It was a matter of sincerity, totally non-metaphysical and genuine. A "Yours and Mine" world and a meeting of souls embedded in each other's existence.[28]

[28] Chisato Kitagawa email. Father Oshida Shigeto, *Tooi Manazashi, A Far Away Look*, English translation by Chisato Kitagawa (Tokyo: Chiyūsha, 1983), 47–74.

Culturally, Professor Kitagawa links Father Oshida's openness to truth and his inclusive embrace of diverse faiths and spiritual traditions to a Japanese reading of the proverbial story of the "Five Blind Men and the Elephant," widely known in diverse cultures and traditions, East and West. Each person's touch leads to a different identification of the object perceived and a dissimilar interpretation. Instead of quarreling over divergent views, a traditional Japanese approach would be to accept and even embrace one another's conclusions in an awareness of a mutual openness to the fullness of reality and inexhaustible truth. This is a distinctively Japanese way of seeing, a Japanese cultural vision, one that Oshida fully embraced.[29]

Beyond these personal and cultural characteristics that illuminate Father Oshida's call to travel, what is central in his vocation is his self-identification as "a Buddhist who encountered Christ." A minor but informative example of both identities melded into one comes to mind. Father Hiroshige Watanabe, OP, points out that originally, Dominicans were itinerant mendicants who begged for what they needed, much as do Japanese Buddhist monks who go on alms rounds, *takuhatsu*, 托鉢, begging for offerings to be placed in a bowl or sack. "As a friar who begged, Father Oshida should have found it relatively easy picking himself up and going for a tour,"[30] Father Watanabe muses. Furthermore, Oshida was certain of his Buddhist-Christian identity and confident of his ability to communicate.

---

[29] Personal conversation between Kitagawa and author. Accordingly, Kitagawa notes, true to his cultural vision and vocation, Oshida looked beyond Japan. Similarly, Joseph Mitsuo Kitagawa, Chisato's uncle who was also an Anglican priest, looked beyond Europe for a truer vision of Christianity. See Joseph Mitsuo Kitagawa, *The Christian Tradition: Beyond Its European Captivity* (Philadelphia: Trinity Press International, 1992).

[30] Father Hiroshige Watanabe, OP, Chisato Kitagawa interview, Takamori Soan; Kitagawa email to Lucien Miller, June 5, 2015.

Most important, he believed that truly vital language is "event language" and not "metaphysical language." He had to meet face-to-face with fellow pilgrims and religious leaders across the world. Everywhere he went he was attracted to the "underground stream" or "subterranean current" (*chikaryuu*, 地下流) he encountered in different spiritual and religious traditions and persons.[31] Father Oshida had experienced that undercurrent flowing within the tradition of the Dominican Order when he was given permission to leave conventual life and go off on his own to fulfill his vocation as a Dominican priest and solitary. That was the starting point of his new life as a solitary and founder of an international community, the hermitage known as Takamori Soan, and as an international pilgrim traveler without peer.

---

[31] Oshida's "Underground Stream" parallels the "flow of waters . . . fountainizing all" concept of California naturalist and founder of the Sierra Club, John Muir. William Frederic Bade, *The Life and Letters of John Muir* (Boston: Houghton Mifflin, 1924), 317. Letter to Catherine Merit, June 9, 1872.

CHAPTER THREE

Poet and Mystic

The essence of Shigeto Oshida's spirituality can be found in the poetry he wrote for *White Deer*,[1] a book of woodcuts created by his soulmate, the Hungarian artist Joseph Domjan (1907–1992). In "Genesis," his introduction to that book, Father Oshida describes his initial meeting with Domjan in a New York forest as serendipitous yet somehow mystically pre-ordained. Their two meetings, which lasted only a couple of hours and were separated by three years, fulfilled a secret need and were moments of grace that nourished his creative spirit.

The poetry in *White Deer* is an eloquent witness to Oshida's free spirit and the sudden mystical moments that he experienced while wandering with "a whistle on his lips." The poems published in *White Deer*, as well as the poetry that years later blossomed from the encounter and the collaborative effort of these two remarkable men reveal the hidden Oshida, his innermost and overarching philosophical and theological vision.

The English translation of Oshida's prose and poetry that follows is the fruit of my collaboration with Chisato Kitagawa. My "Renditions" of Oshida's poems are based on Kitagawa's literal English translations and informed by my knowledge of

---

[1] Joseph Domjan (woodcuts) and Shigeto Oshida (poems), *White Deer*, trans. M. Sato and L. Husain, trans. of Japanese original (Tokyo: The Board of Publications, The United Church of Christ in Japan, 2015). Images of Domjan's woodcuts can easily be found online.

the person and spirituality of Father Oshida. His poetry emerges from a lifetime of prayer and contemplation. According to Father Hiroshige Watanabe, OP, who now directs Takamori, "People say that a deepening process of a life with God in His mystery is depicted here."[2] The narrative sections are taken from "Genesis," Oshida's introduction to *White Deer*, and provide an account of his two meetings with Domjan.

At the outset of "Genesis," Father Oshida tells the reader that his story is not a fairy tale but something that actually happened, a real event, an encounter with a world yet to be. He states that this experience is indescribable and that what he realized from it is beyond human words. Still, he will say what he can simply and plainly.

> In 1974 I needed to participate in several overseas conferences, among them gatherings in the USA. When I arrived at the New York City airport, my would-be guide made an unexpected request: would I perform the wedding ceremony for him and his fiancée who was standing at his side, gazing hopefully at me? The marriage was to take place in Tuxedo Park, a wealthy suburb an hour's drive from the city. The couple were planning to leave their affluent neighborhood and move to Korea where they would be volunteers in social services. I had a busy schedule to follow, yes, but the couple's genuine spirit and integrity touched me and I agreed. After all, Tuxedo Park was a place surrounded by deep northeastern woods in which I had always wanted to set foot, and they agreed to celebrate the wedding in the woods to avoid whatever religious or practical restrictions there might be.

[2] In an email to me, Father Hiroshige Watanabe said, "It seems that several people worked on the production of this book of woodprints as a group effort, starting from the very beginning process of making the rice paper with which the book was made. 100 copies were printed, of which 50 are in Japan presumably, and the other 50 were sent to Domjan. The price of a copy has now soared to as much as 100,000 yen [$975.00], and it is difficult to get hold of. Fortunately, Takamori Soan has one copy, and so we can look at it." Eventually, the original was republished in 2015.

Father Oshida was lodged at the plush Tuxedo Club the night before the wedding. He was all alone. "A person may sleep in a temporal void," he commented.

> We experience all kinds of emptiness in our lives, and we can get used to it. It had often seemed to me that I had lived the last twenty years without finding anyone with whom I could really communicate the depth of my feelings— weighty burdens, the image of unforgettable childlike adoration before beauty stored in my heart, unremitting thinking and searching for the meaning of life. I could take loneliness in stride.

After breakfast the next morning, in the time remaining before the ten o'clock ceremony, he decided to take a walk in the woods behind the house of the fiancée's mother. Among the trees, away from people and passing cars, he walked quietly, musing about what he would say to the guests during the wedding ceremony.

"Suddenly I had a strange feeling that someone was hurrying after me," Oshida recalled. "As I turned around to look over my shoulder, an old man began to speak to me without any word of introduction."

"Won't you please come to my house for a brief visit?" he urged.

"I was quite surprised, especially when he went on to explain that his home was somewhat like an art gallery. Fortunately, I have an adventurous spirit, and he did not look like a malicious person."

"I'm on my way to attend a wedding ceremony but I think I can spare some time," I replied. "As he retraced his steps to his home, I inquired about the kind of work he did."

> "I'm a woodcutter," he answered.
> I assumed he meant he was a lumberjack. But the house he took me to was too elegant for a lumberjack's cottage. When he opened the front door, I was struck with amazement and wondered if I were being bewitched. Feeling confused,

I stepped into the home and stood stock-still. An overwhelming sense of beauty engulfed my small physical
frame like a sudden gust of wind. I felt deeply in touch with
my inner self. Both of us fell silent. Then I stepped forward
boldly into the brilliant light of the beautiful atelier. The
large room felt as though it were alive. The lovely woodcuts
and tapestries hanging from the walls triggered something
deep within. Still silent, I entered the space without saying
a word.

The richness of Domjan's art was in such contrast with the
emptiness of time and space Oshida had endured for so long
that he was overawed. A bird motif on a large tapestry caught
his attention, and as he drew near he told Domjan that the
design reminded him of a phoenix he had once seen on a Per-
sian tapestry near the entrance to the Louvre.

"An oriental spirit flows in your work that is altogether
original," Oshida commented. Domjan pointed out that he
was Hungarian and the bird motifs in his art were Hungarian.
He disclosed that his parents, brothers, and sisters had all
perished in the October 1956 Hungarian Revolution. He, his
wife, and their children were the only survivors. Then he
dropped the subject, refusing to say anything more.

"I somehow had a feeling that I had seen him before,"
Oshida recollected. He began to think he must have seen his
artwork somewhere. Domjan's wife thought that was possible
because he had had an exhibition in Tokyo. Oshida himself
was uncertain—maybe it was the Modern Art Museum in the
Ueno district of Tokyo, maybe not. Domjan brought out a small
book titled *Dürer and Domjan*,[3] and told him about the exhibits
he had had. It then dawned on Oshida that this reticent quiet
man was indeed the master woodcut artist Joseph Domjan
himself. He also had a vague memory of reading the title *Dürer*

---

[3] Douglas J. M. Graham, *Dürer and Domjan: Over Fifty Works by Two Masters
of the Woodcut to Honor Domjan's Two Hundred and Fiftieth Exhibition* (New
York: Graham Collection, 1972).

and Domjan in an art journal when he was a student. Yes Oshida concluded, it was entirely possible he had seen Domjan's art exhibit in Tokyo.

"The man in front of me, however," Oshida avowed, "represented something far greater and far more real than anything having to do with my past memories or awareness of my feelings. I had an intuitive sense that something was about to be revealed."

Speaking about his atelier, Domjan noted that he had designed and built it himself a few years ago after an arsonist destroyed his home and belongings.

Unfortunately after just a half-hour, too little time for a proper appreciation of Domjan's art, Oshida had to leave. The interval disappeared like a breath of air. "Then Domjan spoke to me just as he had when he first called me, inviting me to come again."

Domjan's wife echoed her husband's words. "Please drop by any time. We will always have a room for you."

As Father Oshida left, he glanced at early woodcuts that had escaped the fire along with some later works that were on display and thought of how much Domjan had suffered in the years he created these works.

"Do you feel lonely in this place?" he asked Domjan pointedly.

"Yes," Domjan replied. "You cannot really communicate with the people here."

They re-entered the woods together.

"Why did you decide to call out to me?" Oshida asked.

"I don't know why exactly. Something inside of me compelled me to detain the man I saw passing by."[4] For Domjan it was a moment in which a mysterious wondrous wind had passed through the valley of his profound loneliness.

[4] *White Deer*, 70.

We hugged one another at a fork in the trail. Domjan's eyes were wet with tears. As I walked I felt that Domjan had encountered me more than I had encountered him. He had borne a much greater suffering and deeper loneliness. The phoenix spread its wings wide above.

Return to the Forest[5]

In the late summer of 1977, my wife Bonnie and I together with the New Covenant Community,[6] a small lay group we had founded, invited Father Oshida to lead one of his "contemplative retreats"—his preferred title for extended periods of prayer, reflection, and *zazen*.[7] He decided that he would take this opportunity to stay at Domjan's place for a few days after the retreat at Mary House. When the retreat was over, however, he received an urgent telephone call from someone in the village adjacent to Takamori pleading with him to return to Japan immediately because a motion was about to be forced through a village general meeting to sell the magnificent Koizumi spring to a realty company. There was only time for a one-day visit.

Since the first encounter three years previously, Oshida had not studied Domjan's life and work any further. Sheepishly, he divulged that he had not even brought a gift. In this second visit, they simply picked up where they had left off. It was, in Oshida's words, "as brief as a passing wind."

---

[5] Father Oshida's account of his second encounter with Domjan, like the first, is taken from "Genesis," the introduction to *White Deer*.

[6] The New Covenant Community (1971–1983) was a Catholic lay group founded in the spirit of Vatican II, dedicated to weekly prayer, social justice, service to the poor, and sponsorship of a Vietnamese refugee family. It was inspired by Tony Walsh, Canadian founder of the Benedict Labre House in Montreal, Canada, and Father Mark Delery, OCSO, member of St. Joseph's Abbey, Spencer, Massachusetts, and Abbot of Our Lady of the Holy Cross in Berryville, Virginia. Founding members were Lucien and Bonnie Miller, Sister Jane Morrissey, SSJ, and Anne and Thom Martens.

[7] August 21–27, 1977. This was the first of three retreats or *sesshins* led by Father Oshida that my wife Bonnie and I sponsored along with our New Covenant Community.

When Father Oshida entered the atelier this time, he felt a mystical luminescence. The room was bathed in color.

"Things have changed," Oshida said.

"Yes," Domjan agreed.

Domjan, now seventy, shared his life story. He was born into a poor family of twelve children on March 15, 1907. His father gambled away the family's small income. As a child, Domjan was a dreamer fond of telling stories to his little friends and visiting art museums, but he never imagined that one day he would be an artist devoted to creating beauty. In fact, his father wanted him to be a day laborer. A physical exam required for workers, however, revealed that he had tuberculosis and had only a year to live. Miraculously, he regained his health. For the next several years he struggled to find work during a time of economic depression and attended art schools in his free time.

Deeply discouraged, he lived as a hermit for a year and then walked thousands of miles across Europe, visiting churches and museums and, like Oshida, searching for meaning in his life. At some point during his wandering, he encountered one of the self-portraits of the Italian artist Giorgio de Chirico (1888–1978), founder of the Metaphysical art movement. With that discovery, his life changed.

Standing before the painting he understood that his soul was Giorgio's. That realization was the culmination of his search; his call to be an artist was now clear. Remarking on the phenomenon of religious ecstasy and altered states of consciousness, Domjan said, "I am not a believer in shamanism, nor do I want to be, but I hoped that someday I would learn from a true master what this experience was all about."

Father Oshida felt particular empathy for Domjan when he spoke of his brush with death.

> This kind of ongoing lived event does not remain merely a memory of something in the past but seems to affect one's manner of living. It is not a surprise if there was a distant

echo of his near-death experience in his inner self that
prompted him to call to me on the day of our first encounter. But when he told me of the experience, I did not share
with him my own, nor do I think he would have shown a
particular interest in it if I had. Sharing such experiences
may have led to some level of mutual awareness of where
we had come from. It would not have contributed to a
fundamental understanding of each other.

The fact that Domjan felt compelled to call out to me on
that day is a matter that belongs to a different dimension.
It concerns our inner life, that is, life itself. It concerns the
beginning of life with its light and breath, filling space.
When I stood before his work in his atelier and told him,
"I have met you somewhere before," I did wonder where
I had seen his work and on what occasion. Such a concern,
however, was irrelevant. The instant feeling of "I know
him," of perceiving the shape of the forest in his inner self;
that was the fact that I cherished. Exactly when I came to
know of this forest I have no idea. But it is an undeniable
fact that I knew it.

Domjan's answer to my question was exactly the same
as mine. He said, "I have no idea. It is just that something
within me compelled me to go and detain this person." He
is correct in saying that he did not know what it was that
compelled him to call to me, to cause that event to occur.
The Hand that causes such a thing to happen resides beyond our comprehension. [8]

Mystics call this meeting of souls "spiritual kinship." Harvey
Egan notes that "in the Christian tradition, one . . . finds mys-
tics who resonated instinctively with the holiness of others."
As an example, he points to St. Maria Faustina Kowalska:

Faustina . . . experienced such "spiritual kinship." Often
powerless to describe her ineffable union with God, never-
theless, when she met a person with this same grace, the

---

[8] In a prose piece that follows the above, "Ten-Sided View," Oshida writes:
"When I said to Domjan that I might have seen him somewhere before, I may
have been looking into the forest of my own depths." *White Deer*, 67.

two understood each other extraordinarily well in regard to these matters, even though they speak but little with each other. A soul united with God in this way easily recognizes a similar soul, even if the latter has not revealed its interior life to it, but merely speaks in an ordinary way.[9]

I find these two encounters between a woodcut artist and a cenobitic hermit to be an unveiling of the ineffable, its qualities akin to a mini book of revelation. Two mystics meet, seemly by utter chance. They are brought together by an unexpected wedding and a "Please come to my house" invitation to a priest-hermit-poet from a complete stranger, a "lumberjack" who is actually a famous woodcut artist, painter, and print-maker. Immediately there comes a realization beyond words, never to be fully grasped, more real than reality itself, more important than life as a whole, a near-death experience that can only be recorded or described, but never fully grasped.

This vignette of an instant in time is readily understood by those close to Father Oshida. I dare to say it would probably also be understood by those who knew and loved Joseph Domjan. A true encounter with Oshida was a matter of deep knowing, a certitude of a different dimension, a grasp of the Hand beyond comprehension. In coming close to him, you sensed that your own interior forest was perceived by him. The phoenix spread its wings.

The Flower of Poetry

I now want to turn to Father Oshida's poetry. In it we discover not only his profound sensibility but also mystical echoes of his spiritual union with a soulmate. His poems are ineffable, mysterious, haunting—for me, a book of revelation.

Regarding the evolution of *White Deer*, Father Hiroshige Watanabe points out that Father Oshida's Japanese poems were handwritten in his elegant calligraphic script that invites

[9] Harvey Egan, "Reflections of Saint Faustina," *Budhi: A Journal of Ideas and Culture* 6, nos. 2 and 3 (2002): 189–221.

the viewer to a contemplative reading of the poem. The latest published edition of *White Deer* includes selective English adaptations of these poems by M. Sato and L. Husain. While I respect these English translations, I deviate from them in my English Renditions so as to restore some relevant details given in the Japanese original but omitted in the English version of Sato and Husain. In my Renditions I also hope to convey my understanding of the nuanced spiritual flow of Oshida's poems. The poem titles are my own; the originals are untitled. I express my gratitude to Chisato Kitagawa without whose aid these Renditions would have not been possible.

My limited knowledge of Japanese prevents me from a scholarly exegesis of Oshida's poetry. My Renditions are interpretations that the reader is free to enjoy or reject. For me, these poems are a collage of Oshida's vision of life and reality. Throughout we find hints, images, suggestions of motifs that were most dear to him. We cannot know for certain what he hoped to convey and therefore can only speculate about their deeper meaning.

Is the White Deer, which is legendary in Hungarian folklore, perhaps the hidden Christ? Are its threefold antlers suggestive of the Holy Trinity? Is the new sun Jesus, his bleeding breast the passion? Could the Great Bird be the Holy Spirit? Is the startling image of the celestial moon nestling in the horns of the deer the Virgin Mary?

Or are all these Christian associations beside the point? Am I missing Buddhist allusions or transcultural threads? There is the Voice seducing us, calling us to a leap of faith like the deer plunging over the precipice. The Unborn Sphere is everywhere, as is the Hand of God, the Source, the Absolute, out of which flow the streams of faith, the sound of every bell, and the fall of every flower and leaf. Tiny things, sparrows, know the Way of Heaven. There is synesthesia and the juxtaposition of the abstract and the concrete, water turned to bird and whispering fish, satori in the splitting of the moon in a moment of sadness, the poet born again, steeped in sin and the unspeakable mystery of baptismal washing in every tradition. Everywhere too is the cross and sacrament, gratitude for the holocaust of dust and ashes, the tornado-like union of life and death in resurrection.

Lucien Miller's
Renditions of

Nineteen Poems
Shigeto Oshida

I. Peace Angel

A Voice beyond
heard yet yonder
entrusted to all creation
not just to us

"Spirit sent"
its name in human history
an underground current
passing through every tradition
calling all

In our wood
A flute sings peace

II. Conversion

No call for wonder
water becoming leaf and fish
fruit a bird
fish whispering

The Universe draws the light of stars
carrying the brilliance of the sun

White Deer born in these woods

III. White Deer's Horns

Three Horns
pre-born signs of the Hand of God
One invisible
far beyond
Another with us

The third breathing
bridging

Three-in-One
life giving universe
born from the life so given
weaving frolicking
threads of wonder

IV. Seduced

Bursting with life yet to be born
White Deer cannot but leap into space
embracing and accepting every form
every species

Expecting nothing in return
no need to ascertain
no need to know

Setting out for the life unknown
enticed by the Voice

V. Cross

Taking the rocky path
sharing the sea of sins
my nature like water
steeped in every tradition
immersed in love

Childbirth
    born again
       and again
          and again

VI. Sacrament

High tide low tide
    reality beyond illusion
dipped in water
    hands raised high
blessing and awe
    unspeakable mystery

VII. Traces

Echoing bell
trembling pond
    10,000 forms touched

Beyond the trellis wall
a fragrant flower falls
    heart-and-mind overflow

VIII. Thrice Born

Rustling breeze
scenting my transfiguration
discord becomes harmony
    light grows radiant
Self beyond self
    beneath my feet
        twinkling stars

IX. Field at Night

Shepherd's heaven
    infinite above
far distant from my every thought
    far beyond life's agenda

I breathe deeply the incoming breeze
    enjoying just to be

Holocaust of ashes and dust
    life's oblation

    praise and surrender

X. Encounter

The wonder of it all
the Great Bird flaming
    Jerusalem's consumption

A new sun
hidden in the reborn bird's breast

uniting heaven and earth
   a new journey

XI. Reality

Fire Peacock
   dead yet risen
sunlit suffused body
   shadowed tail

White Deer breathes
   stars flow

XII. Ten-Sided View

Ten ways of seeing
the soft gaze yonder
true vision of the Other Shore

My eyes moist
enduring time and space
trudging up an uncertain trail
my sigh
daybreak's dew

XIII. Passion

Tree of Life
breasting thorns of sin

blood spurts
   desire fades
      fear disappears

bird and beast play
as one

XIV. The Will of Heaven

Tornado whirling
encompassing all that is
life and death as one

Sparrow attended by the sky
we must speak with thee
to understand
the celestial way

XV. Celestial Mary

Gibbous moon riding stars
her face thrice born
soul transparent

shadowed in moonlight
nestled amidst winged horns
White Deer

XVI. Transformation

Holy breath breathes deeply
setting earth and water ablaze
false self's face burns away
God-given life endures

XVII. Awakening

Moon splits
   the edge of sadness
     satori

XVIII. Even in This

Falling leaf's voice
   listen
     the Unborn Sphere

XIX. Current

Stream flow
   white flower's
     bloom

CHAPTER FOUR

Sesshin Part One

Together with members of our New Covenant Community, my wife and I hosted and helped organize three contemplative retreats that Father Oshida conducted in the United States. The first and second took place at Mary House in Spencer, Massachusetts, close by St. Joseph's Cistercian Abbey, August 21–27, 1977, and August 18–24, 1980; the third was held at Holy Cross Abbey, Berryville, Virginia, in mid-August, 1983.

For these retreats Father Oshida followed the traditional format of a Zen *sesshin*, though he refrained from calling it a *sesshin* or, for that matter, using any of the Japanese terms associated with a *sesshin*. Each day there were three periods for sitting meditation (*zazen*), periods for silence, discussion, and work (*samu*); Mass, a *dharma* talk, and, of course, time for meals and sleep.[1]

---

[1] Father Oshida eschewed terminology in general and did not incorporate Japanese Buddhist words when directing retreats for English-speaking Westerners. He called these retreats "A Way of Contemplation." Because the cultural setting, form, and style he embodied were from traditional Japanese culture, especially that of Japanese Zen Buddhism, I adopt its language. Thus: *sesshin* ("retreat"), *zen* ("contemplation," "meditation"), *zazen* ("sitting meditation"), *kinhin* ("walking meditation"), *samu* ("work"), and *teisho* ("*dharma* talk"). The daily homilies and *teisho* were similar in their depth and spontaneity but differed in that generally the former usually dealt with Christian material, the latter with Buddhist. Sometimes he included both in the same talk, but he always abhorred comparisons. There was no formal *sanzen* or *dokusan*, the traditional Zen private interview between teacher and student

At each of these retreats I took copious notes of Father Oshida's *dharma* talks and his responses to the questions of the participants. I simply do not remember how I could have been so skillful then as to write them down accurately minute by minute, but I did. Father Oshida's daily Scripture talks (*teisho* and *dharma* presentations) were given spontaneously and eclectically during homilies and following periods of sitting meditation. Drawing on the notes I took, as well as those of my wife and of a woman hermit who was a devotee of Father Oshida,[2] I have put his talks in chronological order as if they were given over the course of a single weeklong retreat. Intermittently, I include some historical fiction—a touch of imagination reflecting the mood or the moment and echoing Oshida's momentum.

It is of course not possible to "capture" Father Oshida's dynamic mystical presence in words, nor the dramatic visual shifts in emotion seen in his face and body language as he spoke. The beauty of utter poverty and imperfection, simplicity and emptiness in traditional Japanese aesthetics (*wabi-sabi*) displayed in his daily Masses and meditations, the interplay between himself and his rapt students, the tears and laughter and sudden Joycean epiphanies, as well as the irresistible, infectious atmosphere of long silences—these do elude us. But I'll do my best.

Before our contemplative retreat with Father Oshida began, he stayed with our family on Cadwell Street in "the Holy Hills of Pelham," Massachusetts—as I call our homeland—a quiet, rural community of woods, streams, and lovely water reservoirs that dot the countryside like mountain lakes. To those of

---

following sitting periods, but *sesshin* participants were welcome to see Father Oshida individually.

[2] "Hermit friend." This Catholic woman who is a contemplative and close follower of Father Oshida prefers to remain anonymous. She built her cabin in the woods of Massachusetts, heats it with a wood stove, and pumps water by hand from a well. For light she uses a kerosene lamp. She devotes her life to prayer, supporting herself by making clergy vestments and rosaries.

us Pelhamites who love these hills and woods, they are sacred. Founded in 1738 by Scottish Presbyterians,[3] Pelham is about one hundred miles west of Boston. Immediately to the west is the town of Amherst and the college community of Amherst College, Hampshire College, and the University of Massachusetts.

To the southwest lies Smith College, in Northampton, and Mount Holyoke College on the eastern side of the nearby Connecticut River. Pelham has the oldest town hall in this country in continuous use for its annual town meeting (1743–present). It is also the site of Shay's Rebellion (1786–87), in which veterans of the Revolutionary War rose in resistance against economic and civil rights injustices. The rebellion helped bring about the Constitutional Convention of 1787.

During those few days of Father Oshida's first visit with us in 1977, he kept insisting that he was exhausted and did not want to see anyone or do anything other than the forthcoming *sesshin*. As soon as he arrived, however, the phone kept ringing for him, and he happily took calls. There was a steady series of conversations in English, French, and Japanese with individuals who were obviously old friends hoping to see him and also with those who wanted to invite him to give talks and conferences and visit them and their communities.

Respite for Father Oshida came in the form of moxibustion, a therapy used in East Asian medicine whereby burning mugwort (*moxa*, soft, woolly ground artemisia leaves fixed to acupuncture needles or rolled up in cones) is applied at particular meridian points to stimulate the flow of blood and *qi* (氣, "breath," "air," "life force," "life-energy"). Two persons who knew next to nothing about moxibustion—my wife, Bonnie, and our friend, Anne Martens— played at being traditional Chinese doctors and carried out the therapy, using cones instead of needles, burning small bits of moxa all over Father

[3] Charles Parmenter, *History of Pelham, Massachusetts, from 1738 to 1898* (Press of Carpenter and Morehouse, 1898).

Oshida's back, while he, lying on the bed of our guest room, called out directions to locate the meridian points. I stood in the background, giggling hysterically, smelling the moxa burn, and listening to the hoots of laughter welling up from both the two ladies and their patient, as they tried and mostly failed to fix and burn the moxa in just the right spot.

Somehow word got out that Father Oshida was in town and among the calls were invitations from fellow Dominicans who begged him to visit. I drove him to some Dominican locations and sat by amused and somewhat bemused while he engaged in joyous conversation with friars and contemplative sisters. He obviously was "at home."

One day, he suddenly said he wanted to visit the New England Peace Pagoda in Leverett, Massachusetts, a nearby town. He didn't say why. The Peace Pagoda is one of many around the world belonging to the Nipponzan Myohoji Buddhist Order, founded by the Most Venerable Nichidatsu Fujii (藤井 日達 1885–1985), whose members and associates are, like Mahatma Gandhi and Martin Luther King, dedicated to non-violence. Venerable Fujii, or Guruji as he was most often called, taught and lived the practice of bowing in veneration to the Buddha in others, seeking the transformation of heart and mind, of self and other, and inspiring others to realize a higher potential for humankind. During devotions or group walks and pilgrimages around the world, Guruji's followers pray for world peace by chanting "*Namu Myōhō Renge Kyō*," "Glory to the Sutra of the Lotus of the Supreme Law," a phrase from the Lotus Sutra.

As we walked by a meeting room near the Pagoda, Oshida glanced through the large floor-to-ceiling window just as a monk inside was looking outside.

The monk was Gyoshu Sasamori Shonin.[4] Gyoshu rushed outside, and the two very dear lifelong friends embraced in

---

[4] Gyoshu Sasamori Shonin was the organizer of the 1994–1995 International Interfaith Pilgrimage for Peace in which Father Oshida would later participate.

absolute joy, suddenly drawn together in a totally unexpected encounter. Neither had known the other was in the same vicinity. Father Oshida and I then proceeded to walk clockwise around the Pagoda. He bowed repeatedly at various Pagoda locations and effigies, intoning in Japanese what I assumed to be Buddhist prayers and chants as he walked. He was completely at home at this international Buddhist refuge for peace, just as he was among the Dominicans.

Saturday

Informal Gathering

Mary House, at which the 1977 and 1979 *sesshins* were held, was the lovely colonial-styled retreat house across the street from St. Joseph's Abbey. Set amid woods and spacious lawns, it proved to be an ideal setting for Oshida's "contemplative retreats."[5]

The *sesshin* began informally just before the dinner hour on Saturday afternoon, August 21, 1977. We were to keep silence during *sesshin*, including meals and work hours, but this was a moment for introductions and getting acquainted.

The gathering was diverse: a young contemplative woman; a Jewish graphics artist who was a convert to Catholicism; someone curious about "Zen liturgy"; a French yoga teacher; a literary critic and writer; a soon-to-be-ordained Irish American; a parish priest who taught prayer and mystical literature at a Catholic high school; a woman hermit; a middle-aged holy woman, wife, and mother of five children; three aspirants in the way of East-West spiritual encounter; a Jewish couple with a new baby girl and her babysitter; an eager Western Buddhist whose austere athletic physique reflected his ascetic Zen practice; an assortment of Trappist monks from

---

[5] Alas, Mary House closed in 2022 due to the Covid pandemic after over fifty years of being a contemplative retreat center for persons of all faiths or none, who were welcomed by Joyce Thomasmeyer, inspired hostess and superb manager.

St. Joseph's Abbey, including their venerable Vietnamese novice master, Father Joseph Chu-Cong; a university literature professor; five outstanding Canadian members of Catholic religious communities—three sisters, a priest and a bishop—all close friends of Tony Walsh, founder of the Benedict Labre house in Montreal;[6] and an American Dominican sister and exquisite potter, Celeste M. Burke, who gifted Father Oshida with a glazed cobalt-blue chalice she had made from stone powder and had fired for our daily Eucharists.

Among those whom I knew personally were an American Dominican priest, Father Joseph Campbell OP; Russell Keziere a Canadian art gallery vendor and lay Dominican oblate affiliated with a Dominican priory; my former student, Janet Ward, who following her graduation from UMass in Amherst, had recently become a Catholic Worker and follower of Dorothy Day in New York City; and two extraordinary Catholic Sisters of St. Joseph, Springfield, Massachusetts, Sister Jane Morrissey and Sister Catherine Homrok, servants of justice and mercy to poor families and children with disabilities.

We assembled in the living room—what we soon came to refer to as the *zendo*—our sitting meditation space at Mary House. Those who had arranged for the *sesshin* and were hosting the event greeted the guests, and for several minutes we enjoyed chatting together. Where had we come from? Why were we here?

After meeting and welcoming the *sesshin* participants, Father Oshida began to laugh loudly, looking around at the bright and eager faces before him.

Suddenly, it seemed he was peering at me.

"I came because I thought Lucien Miller was someone else!" he chortled, embarrassing me right at the start. I had been so proud of myself for getting the celebrated Father Shigeto Oshida, OP, a distinguished member of the Dominican Order

---

[6] See Lucien Miller, *Alone for Others: The Life of Tony Walsh* (Toronto: Community Concern Associates Ltd., 1987).

of Preaching Friars in Japan, to come our way. I had vainly assumed that he accepted my invitation because I had made a memorable impression on him when I first visited his hermitage and community at Takamori, Japan, in the summer in 1976, on my way home from attending a Charismatic Zen retreat in Taiwan directed by Father William Johnston, who had urged me to visit Father Oshida.

"When I got off the plane in Hartford," howled Father Oshida, "I couldn't believe my eyes. I was expecting to see a different Lucien. I must have gotten my Luciens mixed up!"

Of course, everyone present enjoyed this revelation immensely—everyone except me.

"We all need our humiliations," someone whispered in my ear, trying to comfort me.

Father Oshida then told of his travel experience flying from Japan. On the San Francisco to New York leg of his travels, he had been bumped from his plane. A computer mistake. No one's fault.

"The A-Bomb will be dropped by a computer mistake," he commented. "No one will be responsible. We are in the nuclear age, the era of nuclear madness. Today's world is not real. The devil is our father."

A bell rang announcing the dinner hour.

Father Oshida bowed and left the room.

No one knew what to think. But we did not say anything as we were to keep silence. Still everyone was wondering. Our father is the devil? Didn't Jesus say something about that (John 8:44)? The world is unreal? The A-Bomb will fall via computer error?

The Spirituality of Father Oshida's Sesshin

After our hushed supper, we returned to the now darkened *zendo*, faintly lit by three or four floor lamps turned low. Still no one said a word including Father Oshida who had preceded us into the *zendo*.

We found him sitting stock-still, rooted to his cushion. Perhaps we were supposed to meditate? No one knew what to do.

Finally, a young girl who was a Zen disciple dared to break the sober silence with a simple question.

"I wonder, Father Oshida, if you would share some guidelines for the *sesshin*?" she asked.

He nodded agreeably but said nothing.

After a respectable pause, she ventured another question, this time one that clearly was vexing her. "And what did you mean when you said 'Our father is the devil?'"

Father Oshida nodded solemnly, absorbing her bewilderment.

"Don't read anything serious this week," he began lightly, a glimmer in his eye. "Let go of your everyday consciousness. It is penitential. We feel we are wasting time, but it is important."

He laughed out loud.

"My advice to any of you who are intellectuals is 'exercise two hours a day.'"

Suddenly, changing course, he urged us to pray every morning that we be converted to God's will and be rid of the ego that made us proud of our ascetic practices.

"Remember the question the all-too-human young monk asked the holy old monk," he added.

"What is your secret?" the young monk begged to know.

"Well," replied the old monk. "I don't fast, I don't stay awake doing night vigils. I only do not do what I want to do."

"What he wanted to do was fast and keep vigils. Instead, he did what he did not want to do." Father Oshida smiled enigmatically.

He turned to the young girl's question about the devil being our father, elaborating on his metaphor.

> The devil is our resistance—to change, to mutability, to death, to not doing what we want to do. This week, let the

first movement of your hearts be divine love, not criticism, judgment, or indifference. Embrace your suffering. Say to yourself, "I must have a pure heart so my spirit can go to God. I must be purified." Each morning at the Eucharist, practice awareness—"the Body of Christ leads me to the bosom of the Father. The Blood of Christ gives me strength." And pray, "May the Blood of Christ give me the courage to say yes for yes, and no for no."

As the Scripture says, "Let your 'Yes' mean 'Yes,' and your 'No' mean 'No.' Anything more is from the evil one" (Matt 5:37).[7]

One of the college literature teachers—an "intellectual"— responded graciously, but his interest was elsewhere. "I appreciate your advice, Father Oshida, and your suggestions about the will and prayer. But how do I know my motivations are good? Also, I'm really deeply interested in that mysterious Zen thing, 'enlightenment.' What about that?"

Initially in this question-and-answer moment, Oshida was uniformly cordial, albeit starkly radical. Now he seemed perturbed.

"You can never know with certainty that your desire is pure or good," he allowed. "But there are indications. You wish it. You can taste and smell signs like humility and simplicity. You yearn to be hidden. You are wary of wealth and long for poverty."

"As for your 'enlightenment,'" he frowned, "that's United States of America spirituality: 'ecstasy.' Religion is not something cheap like that. Even enlightenment occurs on the border of consciousness. It is nothing. Forget it at once. If the ego clings to it, it is the end."

Moving away from the abstraction of seeking "enlightenment," he spoke in terms of the spiritual senses, saying that on the path he was teaching, the way of feeling is different; the way of tasting is different.

[7] Translation, New American Bible, Revised Edition.

I suddenly remembered Oshida's remark one day on my initial visit to Takamori in 1976, "Shameful! People talking about enlightenment."

He expanded what he meant by true prayer by speaking of our approach and receptivity.

"Instead of wanting this or that," he proceeded, "our attitude in prayer should be the opposite: 'There is nothing I shall want.' Be a sheep always watching the shepherd. Desire nothing. No thing. No possessions, spouse, children. Be mindful of poverty and brokenness. Real prayer, real meditation, is contemplation. It is being seduced. It is passive prayer—*dhyana, chan,* Zen—passivity by the breath of God."

Elaborating on passive contemplative prayer, he spoke of the kind of consciousness it incorporates.

> This consciousness is not something you aspire to or long for, as in positive or active prayer—for example, the physical discipline of *zazen* or sitting, where you yearn for awareness—but it is given. What you should seek is to disappear, to surrender to God, to his Hand. One feels that someone else is walking, sitting, living, not me. There is some breath, some movement, from the depths. In passive contemplation the sphere of consciousness is both included and transcended. You need someone to check you. You think you are going in a good direction, but usually it is a contrary direction. That is why saints are grateful when they encounter some difficulty.

Our informal gathering ended. Oshida brought the evening to a close with a bow as he had in the afternoon, and off we went to our beds, everyone keeping the silence.

Day One: Sunday

Morning Homily: "It Is Jesus"

Every day before the *zazen* hour with the *sesshin* participants, Father Oshida presided over the early morning Eucharist in his inimitable *wabi* style, sitting on his black cushion (*zafu*) and floor pad (*zabuton*). I had experienced this simplicity in his Masses at Takamori—an atmosphere of Japanese aesthetic beauty blending pure simplicity and poverty—a hand-thrown stone-ground pottery chalice, a wooden floor-board altar, plain white linen vestments and altar cloths, a single flower in a tiny white vase, woodchips readied in a *hibachi* and lit while invoking the Holy Spirit, ashes faintly falling on the worshipers in the silence of Holy Communion, Oshida softly humming or singing a Japanese, French, English, or Latin hymn in a plaintive voice that brought tears to the eyes of the listeners.

Everything in the Mary House Eucharist was the same as at Takamori except for the fire. Our *zendo* lacked the conical hole in the vaulted straw roof that drew smoke out of the chapel at Takamori.

Father gave a brief homily, poignantly elaborating on the realities of our spiritual state as retreatants and on our need to hear the voice of humanity.

> Let us begin with the awareness that "I am alone before God," and "Thou shalt serve no other gods but Me." Let us be shameful before God, ashamed of the noises we make to God, our thinking of how good we are. If we heed the call to disappear to our selves, to make faith our motivation, then we shall see Christ.

He cupped his hands beneath his heart, reached up to the corpus of Christ hanging from the cross on the wall behind him, and opened his hands, as though he were releasing his heart, a bird in flight.

"Place your heart in the midst of the heart of Jesus and let it go," he exhorted us. "Have before you the grief and suffering all over the world." He gestured to the rose in a vase on the table before him, gently took the flower out of it, and, with a nod, presented it as a gift to each of us, one by one. Then, with a bow, he put a fresh white rose in the vase in place of the red one.

"What does John mean when he writes, 'Through him all things were made' (John 1:3)?" he asked, contemplating us.

"Look at the flower. It is Jesus."

He rose, blew out the candle before him, and left the room.

After Father Oshida departed, we sat in dazed silence, absorbing the simplicity of his Mass, our being alone before God, and the shameful "noise" of our ego. As I gazed at the early morning sunlight slowly moving across the hardwood living room floor of our *zendo* in Mary House, a flock of crows called from the treetops of the adjoining pine grove.

What could it mean—the flower is Jesus?

Zazen Hour

Following Mass, breakfast, and simple morning clean-up chores, we met for our first formal sitting. Before the contemplative retreat formally began, several of us participants had arrived early to set up. We transformed the Mary House living room into a *zendo* by removing furniture, rugs, and wall hangings and arranging the *zafu* meditation pillows and *zabuton* mats, some of which were borrowed from monks who practiced *zazen* at St. Joseph's Abbey. We placed them in rows along three sides of the *zendo* walls, and down the center, leaving room in front of the fourth wall for Father Oshida's pillow, mat, small table, Bible, and flower vase.

Each morning before Mass, someone placed a fresh rose from the garden in the vase.

A crucifix was hung in an alcove at the front of the *zendo* behind Oshida's *zazen* location, and at the other end of the *zendo* we placed a beautiful replica of a Bernini bust of Mary, her open hands crossed at the wrist like wings and turned upward in supplication and receptivity. To the side of the *zendo* an exact replica of Georges Rouault's painting of St. Veronica in tears was left suspended above the fireplace. A sitting Buddha looked down from a bookshelf in the corner of the room.

There was an air of excitement among us. For some, this was their first experience of a *sesshin*. Those who had already made a *sesshin* were awaiting a Christian encounter with Buddhism, or a Buddhist encounter with Christianity.

Father Oshida's remarks the day before and during his morning homily were echoing in our minds, as they were to do throughout the week, reminding us that the reason we were here was that we were being called to intimacy with God and self. This was to be our first full hour of sitting. We understood that at some point following this morning's *zazen*, Father Oshida would be giving his first *teisho*, an extempore talk on spirituality or a Scripture text. The daily *teisho* might come any time after *zazen*, in the morning, afternoon, or evening, twice a day. After this morning's *teisho*, we would proceed to lunch.

Before he could begin, however, one of the Canadian sisters could not resist raising her hand and commenting on the morning Eucharist—our sitting in shared silence, the simplicity of clay vessels, the pine board altar on the floor, Father's haunting voice chanting the sacred liturgy.

"Father Oshida," she affirmed, "I felt deeply the presence of Christ this morning in the exquisite beauty of the timeless moment."

Oshida beamed in recognition, knowing she was touched and realizing that she understood.

"Yes," he agreed. "The Eucharist is not time-bound. It engages us from beneath, not from consciousness. Say 'goodbye' to the little consciousness. Cut off judgment. Listen to the Voice of God—the event, the realization that comes, not from outside, but from inside."

There were a few seasoned monks and lay *zazen* veterans among us, but the majority had no experience of sitting cross-legged. Some participants had already felt pain from awkwardly trying to sit during the Eucharist and were wondering how they were going to last the week.

Oshida of course understood that it was difficult for Westerners to sit cross-legged. I had been through two or three *sesshins* conducted by the Japanese Zen master, Joshu Sasaki Roshi, when he had come to Smith College, St. Joseph's Abbey, and Mary House in the past, so I presumed I knew the simple mechanics of *zazen*. But when I began helping people next to me, Father Oshida became visibly irritated. He was the master in charge, keen about everything, especially proper sitting.

Before he began his *teisho*, he demonstrated the important bodily elements of *zazen*: how to cross the legs; the position of knees, hands, upper body, and eyes, and breathing. He went around the *zendo* helping the retreatants maintain the right posture. We did not have to sit in the ideal "lotus" position, with both feet placed atop opposite thighs, but could do a half-lotus, one leg folded on a thigh, the other bent underneath on the floor. We could also sit upright in a chair as long as we remained still.

"Sitting is harmless," he assured us. We had nothing to fear. I noted to myself Oshida had not said that proper sitting would be painless.

He returned to his cushion, rang a bell, and the sitting session began, the first of three hour-long sittings each day. Every hour was to be divided into two twenty-five-minute periods, separated by ten minutes of *kinhin*, meditative walking in a circle in the Mary House *zendo*, or outside.

After what seemed an endless time at the end of our first twenty-five minutes, Father Oshida rang the bell again, cueing us that the first *zazen* period was ended. He bowed, his palms held together in the *gasshō* position as in prayer, and chanted quietly *Itadakimasu* (いただきます), "Thank you." It was the signal for everyone to relax, stretch, stand up and bow, repeating "*Itadakimasu*" before beginning *kinhin*.

One of the two Sisters of St. Joseph attending the *sesshin*, Sister Jane, started teetering as soon as she stood up, and suddenly collapsed in a heap on the *zendo* floor. Trying faithfully to sit cross-legged had caused her legs to fall asleep. When she fell, she sprained her ankle.

Father Oshida and retreatants quickly gathered around, comforting her. One of the monks, Father Mark, was a doctor, and he quickly took care of her ankle, applying an ice pack and wrapping an elastic stretch bandage around a splint.

Father Oshida was most compassionate and a little remorseful. "I have never seen this before!" he exclaimed, wondrously.

"There's always a first time," an American student joked.

After *kinhin*, the second period of *zazen* began, this time without our dear Sister of St. Joseph. The rest of the week she meditated sitting in a chair.

Morning Teisho: *"Sitting, 'The Look,' Breathing"*

Following the morning's *zazen* rest break, Father Oshida asked us to pick up our cushions and mats and casually rearrange them on the hardwood floor in front of his place at the head of the *zendo*. We were free to be as comfortable as we wanted, with legs stretched out or hugging our knees. Keen sitters resumed their *zazen* position. Brilliant morning sunshine streamed into the room through open windows. There was an air of expectancy in the *zendo* and a touch of nervous excitement on our faces.

"Ita-daki-masu," he chanted slowly at the start of his first *teisho*, inviting us to respond. "Ita-daki-masu," we chanted back, a little more slowly, as most of us were not used to the Japanese word he had just introduced at the ending of morning *zazen*.

"It is the customary phrase for expressing gratitude in Japan," he explained. "Before a meal, those eating put their palms together and recite, '*Itadakimasu*' meaning, 'I humbly receive.' It is an expression of giving thanks for all those who play a role in cultivating, providing, or preparing our food."

The *sesshin* thus commenced with gratitude.

Father Oshida began his *teisho* speaking in general terms about ways of supporting sitting practice, emphasizing the importance of proper motivation and leading a virtuous or simple life. He encouraged everyone to reduce daily consumption of meat and alcohol. Then he began to expand on specific aspects of *zazen*—sitting, "the look," and breathing.

"The way to our center is sitting," he said simply. "Sitting is a sign of good will, but it is not simply a matter of will. Contemplative prayer is a gift. We open ourselves freely to receive it without any expectation of reward or pay. The gift is given when it is not expected. We sit with genuine, true sincerity, *makoto* (誠 真). Like the eighty-year-old sister who came to Takamori and piled cushions high so she could sit, and tilted the whole time back and forth, from right to left, trying hard to keep her balance.

"I loved that sister. *Makoto*."

"What about the pain in cross-legged sitting?" a Trappist monk asked. "When I sit, it's pure torture."

"For some," Oshida smiled, "sitting is like acupuncture. The needles overstimulate the nerves so they become numb." His gaze floated about the *zendo*, pausing on each of us. He turned to the example of a father and his child as Sasaki Roshi had during a *sesshin* at Mary House. "Love your pain as a father loves his lice-covered baby," Roshi had goaded me. Father Oshida agreed, but with a difference. "Accept your sitting pain," he adjured us. "The baby is Christ."

> In the silence of sitting, look at the baby you once were with all your weaknesses and tendencies. And look at yourself now. See those same things which have made you what you are. Be with the pain, stay with the pain, embrace that pain, and you embrace the whole reality of Christ.

He stopped for a moment, breathing deeply, thinking about pain. "The truth is," he explained, "when you sit, you are sitting on the cross."

> You must sit there, exist there, and listen. Bear the tears of the world—nuclear madness, the Jewish-Arab conflict, the Vietnam War, the sadness of the Jewish woman who realized Christ was the Messiah, who needed to abandon her family, who married a Muslim. As at Mass, ask for the forgiveness of the world. There are no exceptional experiences. There is only the cross.

After a long pause, he added enigmatically, "Only Christ can sit on the cross."

Before we could probe our hearts, Father Oshida changed direction, turning to two other basics in *zazen*.

"In sitting, both the look and breathing are fundamental," he went on. "Do you remember the look of Pelé, the Brazilian soccer star, or the TV Detective Columbo?"[8]

Oshida pretended to be Pelé trotting down the soccer field, a huge smile on his face as he glanced left and right, his eyes not focused on the ball before him but seeing with a far-distant look.

> Pelé and Columbo, they have the look. The object before them is kept in their awareness, but within the whole. Gazing at a ball, a murder scene, a person, they look far, long, and deep. In his crime solving, Detective Columbo had the same faraway look. When you sit, look softly with your eyes half-shut. See the floor space before you but see the whole *zendo* as well. When you see a flower, or watch your finger move, or look at a stone, experience unity with the source of life.
>
> See the whole area around the stone, the whole landscape. When you look into another's eyes, see the whole person—the baby, the old man, the young girl. Experience unity. Now you will know what charity is. If you live in a state of *dhyana*, deep contemplation, you always have the faraway look.
>
> The same is true when reading the Bible. Read with the look. Don't just see the words, but look beyond them. Transcend consciousness. Our reading must be contemplative. Whether sitting or reading the Bible, how we look is very important. We must always look beyond while keeping the object in our awareness. It's like when you are doing something or talking to someone, and you become faintly aware of a dog barking far away. Near and far are one. It is the sculptor look. It is the look of faith. If you are offended

---

[8] *Columbo*—American television series starring Peter Falk as Columbo, a homicide detective with the Los Angeles Police Department.

easily, you don't have the faraway look. Christ is in everyone—keep the distant vision! Otherwise you risk choosing
yourself.

He stressed breathing as the key to Zen practice, "the indis-
pensable condition for the spiritual life." We must breathe
deeply from the *hara*, the abdomen, just below the navel, each
breath being the absolute breath.

> Inhale slowly then exhale absolute "one," absolute "two"
> . . . absolute "ten." We may become the effortless con-
> sciousness of counting or consciousness may be cut away.
> Let yourself be seduced, led beyond into elemental silence
> where time stands still. A word or thought may come to
> you that is from God. Let it come but do not return to it
> next time you sit. Let it go. Do not cling to an event.

Father Oshida changed direction from human to divine
breathing. He shared a personal moment of, for want of a better
term, what I might call a kind of sacramental breathing, of
breathing the Divine Breath.

> Some time ago I fell down. I was cleansed in a baptism of
> God's breath. My life, my soul was restored, refreshed. "He
> restores my soul" (Ps 23:3). With the breath and silence, we
> enter into the Bosom of the Father. Eventually, become
> Christ breathing in you. This is how I recognize a Zen
> master, by his look and his breathing. Jesus had them both
> when he was carrying his cross.

Convinced by Father Oshida's presentation, we joined his
closing bow at the bell, chanting *"itadakimasu"* with palms
pressed together in the *gasshō* style of thankfulness and reverence, breathing deeply, eyes focusing softly with the faraway
look.

Following the midday meal each day came a brief siesta,
then *samu*, afternoon chores—silent labor being a fundamental

part of every *sesshin*: Mary House cleaning, window washing, dining room clean up, food preparation, cooking, table setting, *zendo* sweeping, gardening.

Some did trail work on the monastery property or in the Mary House woods; others helped a local farmer or dairy family, pitching hay, forking manure, or painting barns.

This first work period Father Oshida joined me and the work party clearing a trail through the woods from Mary House to St. Joseph's Abbey, up a steep grade, a distance of a mile or so.

As we approached the abbey after climbing a precipitous hill, he was breathing heavily and sweating.

"Japan should never have gone to war with America," he panted as he grinned, implying that by giving Father Oshida such a workout, we were taking revenge on Japan for World War II. I didn't realize until much later that the reason he was breathing so hard was not because of the stiff hike and work on the trail but because he had nearly drowned after World War II and lost a lung as a consequence.

Afternoon Teisho: *"In the Beginning"*

A weary yet exhilarated group of pilgrims assembled in the *zendo* after work, feeling the joy of physically working together, getting to know one another through silent communication, and sensing that we were now on our way. With the sound of a tinkling bell we bowed in place and sat down on our cushions, more or less comfortably, to listen to Father Oshida's *teisho*.

In the tradition of a Buddhist roshi, his talk was spirited and spontaneous, flowing from the heart of a master, coming from his intuitive grasp of Christian and Buddhist scriptures and traditions, and his contemplative experience as hermit leader of his contemplative community, the Takamori Hermitage in the Japanese Alps. He ranged over mystical revelations: *dhyana*, the Hand and Voice of God, and rowing to the high seas.

"All religion is *dhyana*," he began.

"Contemplation," "Zen" in Japanese, "Chan" in Chinese (禪). *Dhyana* Zen is the breath of God, the wisdom of God. It is living the life of God motivated by faith. Each person's *dhyana* is completely different. In this same *dhyana* or contemplative sense we speak of the "Hand of God." For the Greeks, the hand signified the slave, therefore John used *logos*, "word," in the preface to his gospel. 'In the beginning was the Word' (John 1:1).

That was the first tragedy. He should have said '"In the beginning was the Hand," or rather, "In the beginning is Hand." People have made John's *logos* into an idea, a word-idea. "What is it?" they wonder. "What does it mean? Is it a work of the imagination?" No, in the beginning is Hand, the Hand of God. Not an idea, but an event.

Everyone was intrigued by Oshida's rendering of "In the beginning was the Word" as "In the beginning was the Hand." A university student asked how the Hand of God was to be recognized in her life. Oshida responded that if she lived without a plan, serving the deep needs of self and other, later on she would be able to look back and see the Hand of God.

The woman could not understand how it was possible to be a student and live without a plan.

Oshida responded, "We sit so we can experience the Hand of God. Prayer is an encounter with the Hand of God. The moving of your finger is the Hand of God, not you."

He asked her to visualize the Hand of God in the flower, and she said she could.

"That is the grain of faith," he enjoined her, "the faith that can move mountains." This Hand was not in the dictionary. "No, it is to be seen, touched, tasted! It became flesh in the incarnation, the multiplication of loaves, at Gethsemane, and on the cross."

"It happens in Mass," he declared. "We must cry for it."

He elaborated on the Scriptures, citing references to "hand" in the Hebrew and Christian Bibles,[9] and closing with a poignant allusion: "The hands of Adonai were also pierced for us," reminding us that Jesus was "pierced for our transgressions," the scapegoat we look upon, whom we have nailed hand and foot to the cross. (Isa 53:5; Ps 22:16; Zech 12:10; John 20:27).

"May the Hand of God lead us to the Body and Blood of Christ," Oshida prayed.

He chose the metaphor of rowing to refer to the movement of the Hand and our encounter with Jesus in the Eucharist. Dhyana life and practice is being led by God to row to the Word-God, the Hand of God, and Jesus' command at the Last Supper, "Do this in memory of me," is specific, meaning direct action.

> If we are to row to the high seas, the bosom of the Father, Christ's command means put your little boat in the water here where you are, the point of real life, and become me, Jesus' unique self. You are the rower; Christ sits in the stern. Gradually, it is not you who are rowing but Christ rowing eternally. Boat-oars-sails disappear, you disappear, Christ disappears. "[I]t is no longer I who live, but it is Christ who lives in me," says Paul (Gal 2:20). Do this. Plunge into the depths. Plunge into the mystery of the Hand of God, which is here.

Oshida rang the bell. Feeling more familiar now with the *sesshin* format, everyone bowed with palms pressed together and recited, "*Itadakimasu.*"

---

[9] Oshida noted that the word hand, Hebrew *yad*, frequently refers idiomatically to the power or capability of a person or group—the "hand of the enemy," "the hand of the Philistines," "the hands of Moses." The "Hand of God" (*yad haElohim*) is a metaphor for Adonai's power and might. It reaches to the uttermost limits (Isa 59:1) and rescues all who call upon him (Heb 7:25). Adonai continually lifts up his Hand on our behalf (Ps 10:12), upholding the righteous (Ps 37:24; 139:10). His Hand is displayed in his liberation of Israel from Egypt (Exod 13:3-16; Num 33:3).

Day Two: Monday

Morning Homily: "Come and See"

Father Oshida broke the long silence that followed the readings for the morning Eucharist.

Now in our world it is really the time of hot battle against the devil. The drama of God is terrible. So evident. So hidden. Poor Peter. Once Christ named him "Cephas" he could not escape anymore. All vocation is this: "Come and see." See Christ in the baby dying in the street. See where I am. We should not live in the comfortable moment, in the world's recognition. Let us do things that are hidden. Whenever we do them, we shall be on the high seas.

The hope of this continent is those who are hidden and suffering. Don't make noises, even for human justice. Only contemplation can bring fruit. Only in a person united with God can you see the spirituality of justice and peace. You can taste if the Holy Spirit is with someone.

You must be willing to climb the cross. Have the courage to die for those who do not believe us. Don't start some movement. Be simple, humble, transparent.

If we play the piano and someone asks us, "Do you play the piano?" and we say "no," that is false humility. But then if people don't praise us when we do play, we are hurt. Imitate the humility of God, his way of doing, which is infinitely perfect. Whenever we do this, we shall be on the high seas.

Take this opportunity of Communion to die with Jesus. It is useless to assist at Mass if you don't die in Christ eating his Body and drinking his Blood in sincere engagement. This makes the Mass meaningful. Such an opportunity comes inevitably if we say "Yes" when we mean "Yes" or "No" when we mean "No," as Jesus taught in the Sermon on the Mount (Matt 5:37).

He paused yet again, this time looking up at the Mary House living room wall above the fireplace, staring intensely at the print of Georges Henri Rouault's painting of Veronica, the woman said to have wiped the face of Jesus with her veil as he was carrying his cross, leaving an imprint of his face on her veil.

Father Oshida seemed transfixed by the painting, his face suffused with pain and sorrow. In her simple, humble, transparent self, Veronica mirrored what he was saying—our hope is in imitating the humility of God.

According to Rouault's biographer, Fabrice Hergott, Veronica is an image of the ultimate suffering of a holy innocent, immersed in sorrow as she tries to comfort Jesus, dying spiritually in communion with him.[10]

Immediately, Veronica's suffering brought to Father Oshida's mind the Mother of Jesus, afflicted with anguish, standing beneath her son hanging on the cross.

"What saves us from ourselves, if anything can, is Christ and the Virgin Mary," he declared.

Morning Teisho: *"The Mystery of the Word"*

On the morning and afternoon of day two Father Oshida gave longer *teisho* since he wanted to speak at length on his concept of language. He began his talk furtively unfolding a portable blackboard and sketching a large triangle, within and around which he wrote various words and phrases and roughed out directional arrows to indicate the up and down movements of active and passive prayer. For example, one could be actively praying using the senses or imagination and then sink into utter silence. Or alone with God in interior silence through passive prayer, one could find oneself chanting a sacred word or saying the rosary.[11]

---

[10] Fabrice Hergott, *Rouault*, trans. Richard Lewis Rees (Paris: A. Michel, 1991), 23.

[11] The sequence from the top of the triangle to the bottom: Common Word>Parrot Word>Black-and-White Word>Third Leg of Chicken>Word-Idea>Word-Event>Wisdom Word> Word-Encounter>Word-God>Unborn

Turning around after completing his illustration, he beamed mischievously.

"All graphs are to some extent the work of the Devil!" he chortled. "Logical abstract illusions. Explanation always includes some evil. But intelligence is the capacity to read into reality the whole of being."

After gazing at his drawing a long while, pretending to find it fascinating, he proceeded to make his pie-slice chart intelligible.[12] He wanted us to be aware of what he considered the dominant way of seeing, feeling, and thinking in "modern civilization," as opposed to mystical or contemplative vision. He focused on three spheres of the word that he delineated on his chart: Word-Idea, Word-Event, and Word-God. The other words he wrote—Wisdom-Word, Word-Encounter, Word-God —are ineffable words about which he rarely spoke. He led with what might be called the "Common Word"—in his mind the problematical sphere of the Word as used in contemporary language, exemplified in the "Parrot-Word," the "Black-and-White Word," and the "third leg of the chicken."

Parrot-Word and the Black-and-White Word

"The 'Parrot-Word' at the top of the triangle," began Father Oshida, "represents the superficial sphere of the word, words we may repeat mechanically like the parrot without knowing what we are really saying.

"The 'Black-and-White Word' refers to the conceptual usage of language, where a single word represents a single meaning or idea." The problem with conceptual language is that "it

---

Sphere>Hand of God. From bottom to top the sequence is reversed. During prayer or zazen the meditator may move from any level up or down to the next level, or to the termination of the entire sequence immediately.

[12] For Oshida's detailed yet confusing explication of his graph, see Claudia Mattiello, "Zenna," in *Takamori Sōan: Teachings of Shigeto Oshida, a Zen Master* (Buenos Aires: Talleres Gráficos Color Efe, 2007), 61–69.

does not allow us to be led into the Mystery of Reality, unlike paradox, contradiction, and metaphor." Oshida declared that only the language of Word-Event conveys "blessed instability." He maintained that a black-and-white sense of the Word is used almost exclusively by so-called "civilized" people, those educated in a Western way. It represents but one aspect of the Mystery of the Word.

The Third Leg of the Chicken

Father Oshida walked over to his blackboard and next to his triangle of various forms of the word he drew a rooster, seen from the side. It was quite well done, with two staunch legs equipped with dew spurs, a puffed-up chest, tail feathers sticking up and out, and a mighty comb. He then etched in "R. L." and "L. L." to distinguish the right and left legs, and then he tried to draw a third leg on the rooster. As he drew and erased, drew and erased, not being satisfied with any of his efforts, he began to giggle. It didn't take long for us to begin giggling, and soon the room was filled with laughter.

"There, you see!" he exclaimed. "Trying to illustrate the 'Third Leg of the Chicken' exemplifies the problematic nature of the Black-and-White Word. Every farmer knows there is a right leg and a left leg of the chicken and that they do not match," he said.

> To us non-farmers the chicken leg only exists in our heads, an abstraction. Thus 'chicken leg' can mean the right or left leg or both legs but in fact it is neither of them. It is a general, logical mental construct, a categorical word or generalization that does not include the experience of engagement. This kind of word cannot carry contradictory meanings and is directly connected to ego-consciousness. We use these words with a sense of self-satisfaction as if we were really saying something.
>
> A serious problem happens when the abstraction "chicken leg" starts walking around: the "Third Leg of the

Chicken." Examples are words that float like dust, abstractions that are mouthed but are so overused as to be empty of meaning—"democracy," "homeland," "patriotism," "freedom," "progress." All humanity should reflect on the fact that such words have brought disruption and crime. Unless such words are referred to a vision of the whole that contains contradiction and are read into bare reality, they make possible any excuse or explanation.

By "bare reality" Oshida was referring to the Unborn Sphere or Ultimate Reality.

Father Oshida paused at this point, arose from sitting cross-legged on his pillow, and walked over to the open window at the side of the *zendo*. He inhaled and exhaled deeply several times, then strolled over to the front of his portable blackboard and scrutinized his handiwork in the morning light—the triangle graph and the handsome rooster.

"Ah-ha!" he blurted out, rollicking with laughter. "The work of the devil!"

Everyone cracked up, joining in the merriment of Oshida making fun of himself.

He resumed sitting wearing a disarming smile, leaving us in silence for a few minutes, meditating on the Common Word. I imagined that most of us were mulling over our everyday language, how disassociated it was from a higher consciousness, a vision of the whole. He continued his *teisho*, shifting to another sphere or vision of the Word, that of "Word-Idea."

Word-Idea

"Reasoning or intellectualization is carried out in the realm of Word-Idea—logic, analysis, thinking," he explained. "It includes consciousness and imagination, the operation of the will, and positive or active prayer that involves using images or symbols. The logic-idea or Word-Idea is meant to purify the Parrot-Word. We play with reason if we stay on the level of simple Word-Idea."

Oshida amplified his sense of Word-Idea.

> Real thought carries within it what is beyond logic—the wholesome looking into mysterious reality. As long as thought carries the echo of what is beyond logic, it is not alien to real life. In an encounter with some unknown reality, if we begin reasoning while retaining our sense of insecurity and uncertainty—all the while seeking the security of understanding—and arrive at the ultimate point of despair, we are somehow prepared for an encounter with a new reality which at that moment comes from far beyond the horizon of our original thought.

"If we endure and persist in the dark tunnel of our research," he continued, "we shall experience Word-Event."

"Simple Word-Idea, playing with reason without a deeper awareness of what is beyond reason, belongs to the world of politicians, preachers and missionaries, speeches and sermons," Oshida declared. "All of them should commit *hara-kiri* (腹切り)," he scoffed, drawing his hand up and down and across his abdomen, as though he were slitting his belly with a sharp dagger.

The *zendo* sitters laughed nervously, wanting Father Oshida to explain himself. "Why such strong words?" someone murmured aloud.

"Why?" he echoed, now standing up, waving his arms and frowning.

"Why? Because they are always repeating themselves, always restating the same words." His voice softened, as though letting us in on a secret.

> The Sunday sermon is a rewrite. Sermons are published and sold. In church there is no Event. So people do not go to church. They prefer Detective Columbo on TV. There is no understanding of the mystery of Jesus. This society is the ghost of the third leg of the chicken. The church is a big third leg of the chicken. Theology is the third leg of the chicken. Anyone can give a sermon. In church there is no Word-Event. No life. People prefer Columbo.

A physics teacher interrupted, looking curious but puzzled. "I do get stuck in my research as you say, insecure and uncertain, but I'm not sure about the 'new reality' you speak of. Is there something missing from my sense of reasoning? Is that 'Word-Event'?"

Oshida postponed further discussion, and we resumed our sitting.

Bell, bow, *itadakimasu, gasshō*.

Evening Teisho: *The Mystery of the Word (Word-Event)*

This evening had a particularly pleasant feeling as several candles had been lit around the *zendo*, adding to its "Japanese" appeal—the classic simplicity of *zafu, zabuton*, and Buddha icon, together with the corpus of Jesus on the cross, Bernini's Mary with her spirit of supplication and receptivity, and Rouault's Veronica, a Holy Innocent worshiping and comforting Christ.

In addition, several of us and certainly the physics teacher were looking forward to tonight's *teisho* with special eagerness. When we gathered for work in the afternoon we could not help talking. Our minds and hearts were collectively wondering about the words at the bottom of Oshida's graph, near the "Unborn Sphere," an apparent allusion to an Ultimate Reality that was unknowable. What could "Word-Event," "Word-Encounter," and "Word-God" possibly mean if they meant anything?

Evidently, Father Oshida had observed our puzzlement, and though weary from a long day, he spoke with extra enthusiasm. Resuming his presentation, he turned to the further dimensions of the Mystery of the Word and the spheres of language. He pointed to the section of his "diabolical" pie-chart that depicted the wisdom word of Word-Event opening to the Unborn Sphere of bare reality and the Hand of God at the foot of the graph.

"In Word-Event, wisdom words purify logic words," he explained, nodding to the physics teacher in answer to the latter's earlier question.

> Real reasoning is fruitful in itself, but even real reasoning is not the whole process of thinking. When we use a word, it is not always the Word-Idea. Word-Idea does not contain the whole. Word-Event carries contradictory meanings and paradoxes. The Hebrew word *hesed* can mean at the same time both grace and shame. When we are living in grace we have peace in the depth of our existence, but in our consciousness we simultaneously bear a feeling of shame for our own existence. Such words are real words for us in Asia. As long as this kind of echo of the Word is carried, even though a Parrot-Word, it is not alien to real life. The reasoning in Word-Idea can be the result of Word-Event, for Word-Event may be transcribed into Word-Idea, but only through abstraction and restriction.
>
> What impoverishes Word-Idea is not something inherent in thinking, but the very fact that we have lost the sense of wonder in reasoning. The tragedy of many modern intellectuals is the absence of the mysteriousness of the concept. When we encounter the fullness of reality, an image or concept comes welling up born within the bosom of our experience. For example, to read what is happening in the mysterious reality of a little baby, our central attitude should be this wholesome looking.

"When a newborn baby first cries," he added, "it cries, 'Wah, Wah, Wah!' No one taught the baby to cry as it does. It cries with the whole of its being, the whole of its existence, 'Wah, Wah, Wah!'"

His baby imitation was perfect. Everyone got it. Someone echoed out loud our thought. "The baby's cry is Word-Event."

"Yes!" Father Oshida avowed. "This is Word-Event, the word of a baby born under the mysterious engagement of the unknown hidden Hand."

He drove home his point with other striking examples.

> When a farmer takes care of his rice-fields, he does not run
> into the library each time something happens. He listens to
> the rice because the rice will tell him that water or fertilizer
> is lacking. The fact of the rice is the Word. The rice speaks
> in a wholesome way, word and event together.[13]

In Japanese, the word *koto* simultaneously means the
event and the word (事 言). In Sanskrit *śabda* meaning
"speech sound" is similar, as is the Hebrew word *dabar*,
which means "word" and "event." However, because of the
deeply penetrating experience of historical events guided
by the Hand of God through the centuries, *dabar* carries the
sense of "Hand of God,"[14] the producer of the Jewish
people's history and drama. "In the Beginning was the
Word" (John 1:1), the Hand of God. Word is Word-Event.
Natural beings have *dabar*. When we stand beneath a
mighty tree we feel its *dabar*, its "weight," its "presence."

Faith is Word-Event. It is a thing to be tasted in the light
or darkness of mystery. For Jesus, the word "believe" is not
a Word-Idea; it is a Word-Event. It means, "Can't you trust
me yet?" It means the real concern of the visible God (Jesus)
for the invisible "us" and a mutual call. Faith is a word that
issues forth from the reality of the unbreakable handclasp
of God's Hand of mercy and our hand—in all our nakedness—clasping the Hand of God with the urgency of trust
and appealing for mercy. Faith is an event.

It is an encounter of two quite different worlds. For us,
it is a trust beyond our understanding, a trust that springs
from a place deeper than consciousness, and from which
one cries out "Yes!" to an altogether different world. We
experience surrender to God, to his Hand. One feels, not

---

[13] As I mentioned above (p. 40), Father Oshida tried unsuccessfully to
teach me the lesson about the "farmer and the rice" Word-Event when he
shouted to me, "Listen to the rice!" on my first visit to Takamori in 1976.

[14] Another profound sense of *dabar* is its human presence. Speaking of
"the natural radiance, the spiritual resonance, the surrounding effulgence of
the person," the late Father Daniel Berrigan, SJ, pointed to the human mani-
festation of the Hand of God. "Three Conferences for the Novices, Abbey of
Gethsemani," *The Merton Seasonal* (Fall 2016).

me, but someone walking, sitting, living. There is some breath, some movement from the depths. Word-Event is always unique. *Koto*. It cannot be repeated in another context, and in itself it is indescribable.

The vase with a single fresh rose on the desk before Oshida suddenly caught his attention. He gestured to it as he had after his first homily, Sunday morning. "Look at the rose," he said.

"The rose is Word and Event. It speaks. It is Jesus."

He paused for a while on his cushion, staring with a faraway look at the floor. We sat there in silence with him, not saying a word or asking an explanation, absorbing the reality of the rose.

"One cannot be sure one has faith," Oshida began again. "Joan of Arc was asked at her trial: 'Did you do what you did by the Holy Spirit?' If she said 'yes' she was finished. She replied, 'I don't know. But if it was not by the Holy Spirit I hope it is.'[15]

"You can only know by the fruits—humility, generosity—or in reading the Bible in the proper way."

He returned to his graph. Pointing to both Word-Encounter and Word-God, he remarked, "Any event embraced here is no longer 'things that are on earth'" (Col 3:2).

Word-Encounter

Advancing into the vast sphere of Ultimate Reality, Father Oshida explained, Word-Encounter comes closer. Word-Event assumes another dimension. Word-Encounter cannot be transcribed into Word-Idea.

Word-Encounter happens when consciousness and subconsciousness are purified and one's being begins to be

---

[15] Actually, Joan of Arc was asked if she were in God's grace. She replied: "If I am not, may God place me there; if I am, may God so keep me. I should be the saddest in all the world if I knew that I were not in the grace of God." http://sourcebooks.fordham.edu/basis/joanofarc-trial.asp.

penetrated by transparency. One hears the Voice. One can never repeat Word-Encounter consciously. The encounter is the encounter with the Unborn Sphere. In the mystery of Word-Encounter, it seems to me that somehow we are already facing the mystery of Word-God.

Word-God

Concluding his discussion on language and the spheres of the Word, Father Oshida ended his *teisho*:

> Word-God is not objective, nor can it be seized by consciousness, but the commitment in faith with Word-God is direct. In Word-God, even our sins will be tasted not only as personal, but as the sins of humanity. Our whole life disappears, transformed into the life of Word-God, life in the bosom of God, the life of mysterious union with Word-God, the Hand of God.
>
> When we respond to what we should respond to with the whole of our being, at the very moment of need, and when after some time we look back towards what has happened, we shall discern indirectly the trace of Word-God, the Hand of God. Faith life is a mysterious entity conceived in Word-God, and Word-God is infinitely beyond our existence. Faith life is the mystery of mutual inclusion through infinite distance. What determines our way of life concretely is nothing but Word-God.

Bell, bow, *itadakimasu, gasshō*.

After the evening *teisho*, some of us resumed sitting, while others got up and walked outside or retired for the night. I think everyone who remained was pondering the spheres of the Word, especially the enigmatic final two that bordered the Unborn Sphere, namely, "Word-Encounter" and "Word-God." Up to then Father Oshida had said relatively little about them.[16]

---

[16] Years later, I felt Father Oshida's "spheres of the Word" brought me closer to understanding the Holy Trinity, Father, Son, and Holy Spirit. In

While a young Zen devotee walked about the *zendo* quietly blowing out the candles but leaving on a couple of lamps, suddenly, to my surprise, Father Oshida returned and sat down cross-legged on his cushion, joining us sitters who remained meditating.

An indeterminable amount of time passed by. It was late as the evening *teisho* had been long, and my knees and back began to throb. I wondered if Father Oshida were still in charge, or what one was supposed to do to end an extra sitting.

Would Father please ring the bell at last I asked myself, longingly? Maybe some of us were going to sit through the night—a practice Oshida had mentioned previously.

Suddenly, a mouse appeared, scurrying up and down the hardwood floor of the *zendo*, furtively looking for something with its beady eyes. It even scampered over the knees of the Canadian bishop a couple of times. No one moved an inch or said a word. In fact, there was something enormously appealing about the mouse emerging out of nowhere in the silence and faint light, from the Unborn Sphere, as it were, having fun with us would-be seekers of Word-Encounter and Word-God. I thought of the opening lines from Robert Burn's poem, "To a Mouse":

> Wee, sleeket, cowran, tim'rous beastie,
> O, what a panic's in thy breastie![17]

"Ah," Father Oshida mused, eyeing the mouse and ringing the bell. "True Self."

The rest of us cracked up and giggling happily went off for our evening rest.

---

contemporary theological language, "In the beginning is relationship." God is a community. See Richard Rohr, *The Divine Dance: The Trinity and Your Transformation* (London: SPCK, 2016).

[17] Robert Burns, "To a Mouse, on Turning Her Up in Her Nest with the Plough, November, 1785."

Day Three: Tuesday

Morning Homily: "The Womb of Mary"

At today's early morning Eucharist, the presider was Father James Campbell, a member of Father Oshida's Dominican Order. He had come to join the *sesshin* from South Carolina where he was serving in the order's Southern Province. He introduced himself briefly.

When he mentioned, somewhat sheepishly, that he had been an American Air Force bomber pilot during World War II and had dropped bombs over Japan, Father Oshida suddenly roared with laughter.

"Aha!" he cackled. "I was in the Japanese Anti-Aircraft Corp. I was shooting at you while you were bombing me!"

The two war veterans hooted and howled, enjoying this unexpected encounter or, you might say, re-encounter. The *sesshin* dissolved into laughter, with all of us lapping up this moment of inexplicable joy that only former enemies could know.

It happened to be the Feast of Mary's Assumption, August 15. After we had all settled down again, Father Jim said that instead of giving a homily himself, he would like us to act out physically our response to the passage from the Gospel of Luke (1:39-45), which describes Mary's visit to her relative, Elizabeth.

> In those days Mary set out and went with haste to a Judean town in the hill country, where she entered the house of Zechariah and greeted Elizabeth. When Elizabeth heard Mary's greeting, the child leaped in her womb. And Elizabeth was filled with the Holy Spirit and exclaimed with a loud cry, "Blessed are you among women, and blessed is the fruit of your womb. And why has this happened to me, that the mother of my LORD comes to me? For as soon as I heard the sound of your greeting, the child in my womb leaped for joy. And blessed is she who believed that there would be a fulfillment of what was spoken to her by the Lord."

There was a long silence. Like me, most of the men must have felt stumped. What kind of body language could I possibly use to "act out" a woman's pregnancy? One woman raised her arms as though welcoming a beloved visitor. A young man cupped a hand behind an ear, imagining that he was listening attentively to Mary and Elizabeth's voices.

Quietly Father Oshida got up from his cushion, wrapped himself in his prayer shawl, and lay down on the floor, curled in a fetal position, a baby in the womb, a Holy Innocent. We were all mystified, wondering what he was doing.

He lay there in silence for some time as if he were sleeping. When he sat up he began murmuring softly in a low voice, seemingly waking up.

> Thank you, Father Campbell. You made me experience the mystery of the pulsation of blood. "Things that are above" (Col 3:2). Jesus was aware of pulsation when he was in the womb. He did not become Jesus just when he gained consciousness. You made me feel the will of God, the original sign of the cross, the flowing of water and blood.

He went on with an admonition that seemed like a disconnect. Could it have been some return from an immersion in Word-Encounter?

"More people would be happier if they were the servants of Adonai," he declared. "If you continue to display your comical consciousness, you will go to the fire. Henceforth you will accept everything, every difficulty, every contradiction, with the deepest gratitude, the deepest silence. Divine silence."

"Then you will be bonded to our Master, Lord Jesus Christ. One day, the window will be opened!"

Morning Teisho: *"War and Peace"*

This morning before Mass Father Oshida had discovered that he and Father James Campbell were both World War II veterans. Their joyous encounter must have triggered Oshida's memory. At the start of this morning's *teisho*, he paused, scratching his head and puckering his lips. Perhaps he was still contemplating the enlightened mouse.

"It was a beautiful day during World War II," he recounted, now standing amid us as we sat on our cushions, turning about and eyeing each one of his listeners, like a storyteller.

> Not a cloud in the sky. A brilliant blue everywhere. A Japanese and an American pilot encountered one another and immediately went into a dogfight, chasing one another, trying to get their guns in line to shoot. They began to do loop-de-loops in the clear sky.
>
> It was so beautiful, such joy.
>
> One waved his handkerchief at the other, and that pilot waved back with his.
>
> On and on they went, loving their flight, thoroughly enjoying one another. When their fuel began to run low, they waved their wings up and down like a teeter-totter, signaling to one another that it was, alas, time to part.
>
> With a wave and a salute, they flew off in opposite directions.

There was a rapturous smile on Oshida's face. A minute or two went by. Then he returned to his cushion at the head of the *zendo* and sat down. He recalled another unusual war story, this time an incident from the Burmese front.

> There was a lull in the hot war of the battlefield. A Japanese musician started playing the guitar and singing in the tropical night. Everyone on both sides listened. The English soldiers also started humming and singing, forgetting everything, the horrors of war, the fact that a dawn assault was before them.
>
> The Japanese and English became a choir—everyone was singing. One by one, soldiers emerged from the dark and embraced one another.
>
> It can happen. Just a little break in the storm can call it up. "Things that are on earth"? (Col 3:2). It's only human?

I wondered if Oshida were thinking of Kurosawa's film, *Burmese Harp*, but I didn't ask.

"Don't confuse the psychological with the spiritual," he broke in, returning to an earlier theme.

> What is evil is the fact that the human being tastes every-
> thing on the level of consciousness. There is a foul taste in
> the mouth when we do not tell the truth of ourselves before
> God, when we make excuses, audible signs of lies rooted
> in childhood, rooted in Adam and Eve. When we go to
> confession, the examination of conscience is not an abstract
> knowledge of our sins. "I said something three times
> against charity, against my sisters."
>
> In reality, I carry the death of my friend, a martyr, within
> me as the mystery of Jesus. My friend was a volunteer.
> Always in war it is the best boy who goes. So my friend
> who made a prayer not to kill anyone he did not hate, but
> to be killed instead—he volunteered and died.
>
> This is a matter of faith. "Things that are above." Blessing
> and simplicity mean my tasting on the level of the mystery
> of Jesus. It is not a matter of morality. If it were, Jesus would
> never have been killed. Nuclear energy is the challenge of
> the devil. If it were not, I would not have talked about it
> Sunday when we first met.

"The devil is washing our brains making us think that nuclear energy is a very good thing," he declared. "It is a Word-
Idea divorced from Event, the Hand of God. We are in the day
of judgment. 'But woe to you, scribes and Pharisees, hypocrites!' Jesus cries out. 'Woe unto you, blind guides'" (Matt
23:13,16).

After a long silent pause, Oshida remarked. "The founder
of a Catholic school once confessed to me that 'Christian' was
a word he did not like, for it had become contaminated. We
have slaughtered in the name of truth and the church. A completely contaminated word."

Bell, bow, *itadakimasu, gasshō*. Standing up, his head hanging, our storyteller left the *zendo*.

Afternoon Teisho: "East and West"

After the sitting hour, Father Oshida rang the *zendo* bell. A summer thundershower was falling, pounding the Mary House roof. We bowed, stretched our legs or stood quietly, then resumed sitting informally, enjoying the sound of the rain.

He must have known that the Mystery of the Word was very much on our minds—language as event rather than as explanation,[18] which seemed to him to be a basic distinction between East and West, but instead of an elaboration or shared dialogue, he gave a *teisho* about something altogether different. He stood for the whole *teisho*, as if he were giving a sermon or presenting an argument in court. He appeared distressed, as though bearing a burden from which he wished to be delivered.

"I am a Japanese, a Buddhist, who has encountered Christ," he began.

> In both words, ' "Buddhist" and "Christian," I feel some kind of lack. Jesus says "Salvation is from the Jews" (John 4:22). He declares that the time has come when one adores the Father in "Spirit and bare reality" (John 4:23 "in spirit and truth"). According to Jesus, is something like Christianity possible? Christianity as compared to Buddhism? Is it for this that Jesus died?

"What is the horizon towards which Jesus gazed?" he went on, striding up and down, and from one side of the *zendo* to the other.

> If the so-called "followers of Christ" today insist that their task in East-West dialogue means you compare yourselves to others, is this the sign of the New Horizon of bare reality? Each way should be unique, a unique way to the *very him*, to himself, not to man in general.

---

[18] Chisato Kitagawa observes that, for Father Oshida, language as explanation is an evasion, a cop-out.

In every religion it is the same—each one is unique. Shakyamuni Buddha and Dogen Zenji and others—each is unique. The sutra—the canonical Scripture—in other traditions is another kind of revelation. Don't compare! Don't say, "I am superior." Learn other mystical currents. We should adore by Spirit and bare reality. Don't condemn! Don't compare!

He paused, frowning, as if listening to counter-voices.

"It is true, even in Buddhism," he acknowledged, "there is pain, vain talk about 'enlightenment' as though enlightenment were a uniform one could put on."

And then there is the problem of the koan. Buddhists and Western followers of Buddhism are attached to the koan because they lack any real sign of tradition. If they do not have sub-currents it is better for them to disappear. The koan is the occasion to cut us off. "If you have faith, you can move mountains" (see Matt 17:20) is a koan. It cuts through! The bonzes do not know the reason for the koan. Therefore the bonzes cannot satisfy. A flower can be a koan. A great master, Gutei, made a koan of his finger.[19]

He raised his right index finger, cutting the air, as he said this, alluding to the Zen koan, "Gutei's Finger," the story of a boy who began imitating his master, Gutei, by rising one finger whenever there was a Zen discussion. One day, Gutei suddenly cut off the boy's finger, and when the young disciple ran away, the master called him back and raised his finger. When the boy saw Gutei's finger, he became enlightened.[20]

---

[19] Oshida here uses "bonzes" in a rare pejorative sense. He means those Asian or Western Buddhist monks and practitioners who are inept in their koan meditations and get nowhere, unlike the great Zen Master Gutei who in raising his finger brought his young student to immediate realization.

[20] Gutei story from *The Gateless Gate* (*Mumonkan*), a compilation of thirteenth-century classic Zen koans.

"So graphic, so radical," a woman sitting next to me offered. On my other side a man groaned as he released his knee.

Father Oshida nodded but did not respond. Nor did he explain the koan. The rain shower stopped and sunlight streamed into the *zendo*. With this change in the weather he shifted to a singular, contrasting image in the Judaic-Christian tradition, the Hand of God.

"The Hand of God is the specialty of the Judaic-Christian tradition," he affirmed, surprising me. It seemed he was about to draw an East-West comparison, something he usually shunned. But, in fact, it was not so much a comparison as it was an assertion of unity in difference.

> What the Zen masters point to, the divine life, is what we can see in the Scriptures, in the historical Christ. For example, a mystic who was not Christian once said to me, "Jesus did not die on the cross. He was in *samadhi* (deep meditation). It is just a story."
>
> For us Christians, however, every fact is a story. Every fact on the phenomenal level, if seen from the level of the Hand of God, is story. There is no distinction between fact and story. It is what we contemplate. Our contemplation does not exist apart from history.
>
> So, our attitude to history is different. The historical fact is the very place of religion. If story replaces fact, history becomes less important. Christ on the cross is a fact. His crying. It is Incarnation. It is the Hand of God incarnated. Truth there is event.

He checked himself for a moment, searching for an example to illuminate what he was saying. He placed his hands on the low table before him, bowing over in meditation. Then he turned to a Word-Event, a real-life encounter in Bangladesh.

> A Buddhist leader in Bangladesh named Ananda—a person like a bishop—invited me to visit an orphanage. Bangladesh is now full of orphanages. Bishop Ananda then took me on pilgrimage to a Buddhist temple and introduced me as

Christian and Buddhist. A man there, a Buddhist theologian, assumed I took myself to be in fact both a Christian and a Buddhist.

He looked at me and exclaimed: "How disagreeable. You have one leg in one boat and one leg in another. You will fall into the water," he predicted.

"I have been in the water from the beginning!" I exclaimed.

Yes, I agree that the boat is important. But I have been swimming in the water from the beginning. I worship "in the Spirit and in truth" the word of Jesus. It is not the sphere where you compare religions. That is phenomenological.

Bishop Ananda exploded with laughter. He lives in the bottom sphere of event and encounter. He is really Buddhist. He actually tastes who I am. We both respect one another's context. We do not fight. It is not necessary. We respect the mystery of each one. Similarly, there is mutual respect, the basis of peace, between me and Sri Swami Satchidananda, the founder of Integral Yoga.

I have been asked by Buddhist monks to teach the Bible and lead *sesshin*. They do not think this strange.

If Buddhists and Christians are true to their respective teachings, they will embrace one another. If Jesus is the Son of God, not the founder of the phenomenon of Christianity, he should not be regarded as someone of earthly religion. Being true to our respective teachings is freedom, bare reality, and spirit. Without this sense, the basis for peace and humanity is practically impossible. The history of the world in the name of religion is a tragedy and a comedy.

Bell, bow, *itadakimasu, gasshō*.

After his critique of shortfalls in both Christian and Buddhist practice, Father Oshida looked emotionally drained. He had expended himself recounting his pilgrimage as a Buddhist who encountered Christ. In his previous revelation of his spiritual pilgrimage, it was clear that he had found it exceedingly difficult to endure the European-style Christian church that had come to Japan with the Western missionaries. To be true to his Catholic faith and his vocation as a Dominican priest, he had had to become a hermit in the Japanese Alps and the founder of Takamori Hermitage.

Evening Teisho: *"Catholic Suffering"*

Father Oshida's comments about the contaminated word "Christian," his prophetic declaration that judgment day was upon us, and his reference to Jesus' condemnation of hypocrites triggered deep feelings about the present state of the Roman Catholic Church. Moreover, a few lay women and Catholic sisters were piqued by a comment he had made that women in Japan had specific roles and social positions. From their feminist perspective, his statement sounded like an affirmation of the old Western adage that "a woman's place is in the home." Realizing that they were unfamiliar with Japanese culture, they did not, however, say anything directly to Father Oshida.

Listening to Father Oshida's words about the Catholic Church and what it means to be a Christian touched an even deeper nerve. His outspokenness was in such sharp contrast to the gentleness that was so apparent in the way he experienced the pulsation of Jesus' blood in Mary's womb or in his stories about moments of deep peace between wartime enemies and his experience of the mystery of Jesus in the martyrdom of his boyhood friend.

Evidently Father Oshida was aware of our reaction to his *teisho*. Five minutes after we entered the *zendo* and began *zazen*, he rang the bell and asked if we cared to share what was on our hearts and minds. He would speak on a later occasion. He just wanted to listen.

On the faces of some of the clerics and professed religious there was a look of pain. One Canadian nun was weeping. "There is such a weight in being Western," she demurred, "in being Catholic, a religious sister or clergy person. We have done wonderful work in our missions and apostolates abroad, and work with First Nations and Aboriginal Canadians in Canada, but we have destroyed so much of their cultures too. I am going to live with that weight all my life."

"Father," blurted another sister, "there is something else I have to say. Yes, we have done harm," she demurred, "but much good too. Why are you so critical of the Western church? So one-sided. Can't we ever do anything right?"

Oshida listened attentively to both women, absorbing a confession and a complaint, and grimaced upon hearing he was one-sided. He bowed deeply, his palms joined in honoring the sisters' heartache and candor and the shared sense of agony and frustration among religious and laity. He was stunned by a confession of collective guilt for the harm caused by the Western church.

"I have never heard these words before," he said, with both a smile and look of astonishment on his face. "Until now we in Japan have not heard these things. The missionaries say to us, 'We have the truth.' This is heartening and enlightening. Something could begin from this awareness."

Turning to the weeping sister, he said, "Your suffering because of the church is not mistaken. No. It is important for the church, and for you. Keep listening to Christ's own pure voice."

Father Oshida then closed the discussion with two brief stories.

Once an African bishop and I were on an elevator together. He was a simple good man.

"Father," he said to me, "What is prayer? I don't understand."

"The most important thing," I said, "is the first movement of the heart. It must be sincere."

"And if it comes with the second movement of the heart, is that all right?" he asked.

"Yes, it's all right," I answered.

We had arrived at our floor and were standing in the corridor. He made his confession. He confessed not out of duty but because he felt remorse. This was the very first time for me: the presence of someone who wants to confess. The church should restore this sense of simplicity.

Another time I visited a group of people who were literally poor, an Ethiopian church. There were around two hundred persons, including eighty monks and thirty nuns. They had converted to Judaism in the time of Solomon, and later surrendered to Jesus. Their liturgy was very different, with sutras and the popular songs of farmers. There was great sincerity. The oldest monk served us. They are my great consolation.

There are many mystic currents serving Christ: Ethiopian, Coptic, Greek. Don't be afraid to send a young man to other currents of spirit and truth. Don't make comical contemplation. We seek human perfection. But what we should seek is the perfection of surrender.

Bell, bow, *itadakimasu, gasshō.*

After everyone had left the *zendo* for the evening, I remained behind.

Seeing others' tears, I thought of a particular kind of suffering that grieves numbers of faithful Catholics I know, people who remain in the church despite the transgressions of clerics who touch sacred things without any sense of reverence. These people may or may not be conscious of their redemptive role for priests who have abused children and for those laity who have left the church.

They are well versed in what St. Jane Frances de Chantal (1572–1641), called the "martyrdom of love."

One day when addressing her community of the Daughters of the Visitation that she and St. Francis de Sales had founded, she explained that this kind of suffering comes to those who give themselves fully to God and lasts a lifetime. Asked by one sister what this kind of martyrdom was like, she responded, "Yield yourself fully to God and you will find out! Divine love takes its sword to the hidden recesses of our inmost soul and divides us from ourselves."[21]

When my eldest daughter, Anita, was a little girl, she once asked me as we were walking back from a Mass we had attended at a large New York church, "Daddy, do you know why I love the church so much?"

I felt proud. "No," I answered. "Why do you love the church so much?"

"Because it's so crummy!"

She meant it was a hodgepodge, a heterogeneous mix of imperfect souls, persons rubbing up against one another, rich and poor, drunks and street-people, making gems out of grindstones.

I think of this kind of love as "Catholic suffering," a tribulation peculiar to Catholics that Father Oshida was deeply and personally aware of. For all I know, it is a cross for a minority of faithful Catholics throughout the world who worship side-by-side with those laity and clergy who are secure in belonging to an institution but insecure vis-à-vis the gospel's radical call to nonviolence and service to the poor—those who, as Pope Francis reminds us, covet power-over instead of Jesus' model of power-with. The cross of "Catholic suffering" becomes even heavier when clergy who, oblivious of their interior shadows, impose a "Father knows best" clericalism on their congregations.

For Catholics who persist in being part of the apostolic community of faith there is, of course, the ever uplifting and triumphant grace of "Catholic Joy" that Jesus promises us—"I have told you this so that my joy may be in you and that your joy may be complete" (John 15:11)—and offers us in the sacraments: baptism—there is an Other; confirmation—there is no Other; Eucharist—becoming the Other.[22] Above all else,

---

[21] Divine Office, Jane Frances de Chantal, Religious, December 12.

[22] Thomas Keating, *Reflections on the Unknowable* (New York: Lantern Books, 2014), 110–11.

community and communion, the Real Presence of Jesus in his Body and Blood, ignited by the Holy Spirit.

As Pope Francis writes so eloquently and with such delight, there is "The Joy of the Gospel" that never leaves us but calls, stretches, and comforts us again, and again, and again.[23]

Day Four: Wednesday

Morning Homily: "The Character of Jesus"

After the gospel reading at morning Eucharist on Wednesday, Father Oshida bent down as if he were studying patterns on the hardwood floor before him. After remaining deep in thought and prayer for a good while, he sat up, raised his head, and gazed around the *zendo*, studying each of our faces. He seemed to be searching for something, an awareness of individual needs perhaps, or possibly a way to respond to the previous day's confrontation with Catholic suffering.

"Do you know the character of Jesus?" he asked rhetorically, as though inviting us to participate in his homily.

Several people, myself included, nodded, or tentatively raised their hands in affirmation. "We know Jesus," we seemed to be saying.

But no one said anything, all except for a beautiful young woman sitting devotedly right in front of Father Oshida. She had shoulder-length, auburn hair and wore a loose fitting indigo colored smock.

She spoke what most of us were thinking, I'm sure.

"We want to hear what you were meditating about just now," she stated intrepidly. "My guess is it was the character of Jesus."

"Once in France there was a miracle," he recalled, smiling at the redhead's boldness, "a curing of a cripple. It was not my

---

[23] Pope Francis, *Evangelii Gaudium: The Joy of the Gospel* (Washington, DC: United States Conference of Catholic Bishops, 2013).

doing. I felt indifferent to it. It was the work of Christ. I experienced the cure and it was painful. My hand hurt for a month."
He continued,

> Another time, I knew a suffering girl who had dedicated her life. I recalled my experience of being cured in France. I wanted to console this girl. I wanted to apply my hand to the sick part of her body. I did it for three days without result. Somehow she was relieved. I became infinitely tired. I received her sickness. I understood then I should give up. It was above my power. Still she suffered. I must obey what is given. I began to taste the temperament of Jesus. A man who received the sufferings of others. He stooped, he bent down, he was poured into them spontaneously. The Hand of God moved when he received their suffering.
>
> "Who touched me?" he asked when a woman who had been hemorrhaging for twelve years was cured when she touched the tassel of his garment. (Luke 8:45-47) This healing was not initiated in his consciousness. Jesus was open to the sufferings of others.
>
> As for me, the strength of spirit went out from me. I felt it when I began to feel the refusal. It was not for me to receive the sufferings of others. I began to feel Jesus. It was Jesus who cured. "Will you give me a drink?" says the thirsty Jesus to the Samaritan woman at the well. In a moment it is she who thirsts for his "living water."
>
> She asks, "Sir, give me this water, so that I may never be thirsty or have to keep coming here to draw water" (John 4:15). He receives her need. It is Jesus. It is his temperament.
>
> Jesus himself never acts by principle. There are no general principles except in the Word-Idea realm.
>
> For a samurai, the greatest crime would be to go to the phenomenon, the consciousness level, for an excuse. He must be in service to the Event-Life.
>
> Jesus responds to the need, to what he sees. He is a man made to be seduced by the sufferings of others.

The dumb silence in the *zendo* was palpable, overwhelming. What would it mean were each one of us to find others' suffering irresistible?

Father Oshida closed his palms with fingers pointing out to us as we bowed in gratitude; he then sat back on his cushion. Our two Dominican retreatants, Sister Celeste Burke and Father James Campbell, came forward bearing the wooden plank altar to set up for Mass, together with candles, a rose, altar cloths, and the blue chalice Sister Celeste had made.

Morning Teisho: *Reading Scripture*

When we returned to the zendo after morning *zazen*, Father Oshida reminded us of what he had told us at supper the previous evening: this morning's *teisho* would be longer. We bowed, stretched, then took a more relaxed position on our *zafus*, listening to Father's introduction to the Scripture texts for the Mass as he stood before us or walked about, in the semblance of professor and teacher.

He began by speaking about the Bible in general, standing motionless, temporarily rooted to the spot.

"This morning," he said with a grin, "I want to teach you how to read."

> When we read Holy Scriptures, it is a *dhyana* moment.
>
> The Word of the Bible is essentially Word-Event, and it should be treated as such. Don't divide the gospels by chapter divisions. Psychologically we are affected by chapter divisions. As long as we approach the Bible as Word-Idea, we shall never be able to penetrate it. For real life, we continuously have to cut out all abstract reasoning combined with vain explanation, self-satisfaction, self-presentation and self-consciousness, together with all other movements of the ego that appear in our desires. One should really increase silence to taste the Holy Scriptures.
>
> "In the beginning was the Word, and the Word was with God, and the Word was God. He was in the beginning with

God. All things came into being through him, and without
him not one thing came into being. What has come into
being in him was life, and the life was the light of all people"
(John 1:1-4).

"Him," the Word, *logos*. Not Word-Idea but Word-Event.
When Jesus calls his disciples, he calls them by name! It is
Word-Event. If we advance in deepening silence, we will
become more sensitive to Word-Event and will experience
it.

He strode back and forth vigorously between the nearby
zendo window and the library alcove, as if to dramatize the
Word-Event of naming. Then he went on.

Reading the Bible is an adventure into the drama of God.
It is not for understanding. Carry the most difficult passages within you. Don't read commentaries. Someday God
will reveal his Word to you. In reading the Scriptures, seek
what is behind the words of Christ. Don't read them as
mere human words. You must get beyond meaning. Participate in Christ's voice and spirit.

Remember Pelé gazing at the soccer ball, seeing the
whole. The new horizon of humanity would be this look;
without it, we can never pass beyond the crisis we are in.
We are co-responsible for this crisis.

To remain in this look, be poor, be free of any kind of
attachment. If you have the look, your every gesture will
call forth God. To read the Bible is to taste it, to see directly
the Hand of God. The Bible is written from an experience
of the beyond. Saint John the Evangelist felt this. He suffered it. This is what is essential. Taste the Bible from
beyond.

"Don't be attached to the literal word of the Scriptures or a
God concept," he said—this time standing still once again.

The Scriptures were written to express the Word-Wisdom
of God. In my case, I read the Scriptures with rice farmers

and burned the commentaries. To read Holy Scriptures, sit, sit, sit; walk, walk, walk; fast, fast, fast.

For the gospels, start with the last word and read backward. Pick up the comments that only this evangelist makes. These show the writer's vocation. If the comment is more or less the same as in another gospel, watch for a different word or a different way of saying it.

The key to a gospel is the passage that seems strange and is the most difficult to understand. Remove titles and subtitles. Don't divide the gospels into chapters.

Read and taste the echo from one part to another. Where has the writer begun to write again? Each author is writing out of one fundamental vision and contemplation of eternity. The writer writes because he is obliged to write; he must confess. It is the person of Jesus that obliges him to write.

Why? The reason is beyond the reporter's grasp.

The Synoptic Gospels—Matthew, Mark and Luke—are a record of personal experiences of an event. "Synoptic," meaning seen together, with the same eye, implies that these gospels are all the same. No! Each report, each gospel, is unique. Exquisitely unique. Its secret is revealed in the last word of the risen Jesus, a koan.

Matthew's secret for instance is revealed at the end. "I am with you always, to the end of the age" (Matt 28:20).

Knowing this final word, read backward to the beginning of Matthew, the "genealogy of Jesus" (Matt 1:1-17). It is not about genealogy; it is a God-with-us, genealogy by the mercy of God. The author is tasting and seeing. It is a real vision that embraces him. Matthew is a deep mystic, a Jew with Torah in his blood. The Torah is the way to be united with God. He knows the New Torah in the Sermon on the Mount, the echo of Moses.

It is Word-Event. Always, God-with-us.

Mark too, recounts Jesus in his own way. Grasped by the Hand of God, he is very sensitive to the movement of the Spirit of God and the simultaneous movement of the spirit of the devil throughout his narration. For Mark, to be with Jesus is a different existence.

Only Luke has Mary's canticle, her psalm of praise. "All generations will call me blessed," she sings (1:48). He is very gentle to the ladies, showing Jesus curing several of his women followers and providers of their infirmities and evil spirits, including Mary Magdalene, Susanna, and Joanna (Luke 8:2-3). Luke alone tells his beautiful unparalleled story of a rich family's Prodigal Son (Luke 15:11-32).

Why? Because he himself knows the psychology of the sinner.

Each gospel is distinct. The Synoptic theory of fragmented sources is made up by commentators who never pastured sheep or fished in the sea. It is the third leg of the chicken. If God blesses the church, it is not because of these analysts, but because of the hidden suffering poor.

Several of us raised our hands, wanting to ask questions about the three Synoptic Gospels, but Oshida apologized. "I'm so sorry," he said. "Our *sesshin* is only a week long, and already it is Wednesday morning. Tonight after sitting meditation, we need to turn to the 'contemplative gospel,' the Gospel of John."

CHAPTER FIVE

Sesshin Part Two

As I did in the preceding chapter, here too I draw on the three *sesshin* that Father Oshida gave in the United States of America and in which I participated, arranging his teachings as if they were given in a single one-week *sesshin*. This chapter features the homilies and *teisho* that he gave on the Gospel of John.

Day Four: Wednesday

Evening Teisho: *"The Dhyana of John"*

After the bell closing the evening sitting and a brief interval of rest, we reassembled for the evening *teisho*. Coming in to the *zendo* and making our bow, most of us must have noticed a new object on the table beside which Father Oshida was sitting. Along with the usual candle, flower, and Bible, there was a long, black leather pouch shaped like a tube with a zipper running from end to end.

I had no idea what it was, nor probably did anyone else.

As he had promised he would do when he spoke to us this morning Father Oshida turned to the Gospel of John. He began with the death of Jesus, saying, "Everything in John is written in the light of the blood and water John saw flowing from the side of the crucified Christ.[1] As he looked at his Beloved

---

[1] Oshida assumes the traditional identification of the author of the gospel as John. Contemporary biblical scholars maintain the writer is the unnamed

Disciple from the cross, Jesus was in the same state as he was when he was in the pulsating blood and water inside the womb of Mary, the original sign of the cross. He was looking at John from the depths of his existence."

He picked up the Bible lying on the desk before him and read from the Gospel of John line by line, slowly and solemnly.

"Since it was the day of Preparation, the Jews did not want the bodies left on the cross during the sabbath, especially because that sabbath was a day of great solemnity. So they asked Pilate to have the legs of the crucified men broken and the bodies removed" (John 19:31).

Father Oshida's voice became almost a moan. He paused, catching his breath before going on.

"Then the soldiers came and broke the legs of the first and of the other who had been crucified with him. But when they came to Jesus and saw that he was already dead, they did not break his legs. Instead [here he broke into a faint whisper], one of the soldiers pierced his side with a spear, and at once blood and water came out."

Father stopped here and gently looked at each of us one by one, his eyes holding ours, clouding with tears. After a short pause, he dispassionately concluded the passage: "He who saw this has testified so that you also may believe. His testimony is true, and he knows that he tells the truth" (John 19:31-35).

"Usually in the Bible the most difficult part is the most important," Father Oshida observed. "This is the place where Jesus remains in the bosom of the Father. It was John's enlightenment, his *dhyana*. When he writes, it is with one vision from beginning to end, a slideshow, wherein the slides do not unfold one after the other in linear fashion, but each slide is atop the other, a single picture."

I raised my hand, wanting to understand.

"Beloved Disciple" and unidentified "eyewitness" or one of this person's disciples.

"I don't get it," I admitted. "How can you make out any-thing if the slides are merged?"

Father Oshida turned toward his table and picked up the mysterious black leather pouch with obvious glee. He un-zipped it from end to end and brought forth a long silver tube with a viewing aperture at one end and a circular piece of glass on the other.

"Look what I found in my room!" Father Oshida called out.

"A kaleidoscope!" a chorus of retreatants declared. Appar-ently, a previous Mary House guest had forgotten the kaleido-scope and left it in the downstairs bedroom Father Oshida was using.

He put the aperture to his eye and started twisting the tube back and forth and round and round, producing a near infinite pattern of symmetrical mosaics by way of the multiple reflec-tors and colored pieces of glass inside, "Ooh"-ing and "Ah"-ing as he went, with childlike joy at his wondrous discovery.

Gradually, individual sitters began nodding to one another, sharing smiles as they "got it." Instead of writing a chrono-logical narrative, one section leading to the next in a sequential time sequence, John was composing a series of vignettes, in-dividual scenes, settings, and dialogues, as in a memoir, one vignette placed on top of the next, reverberating and resonat-ing with another, causing the reader to see a simultaneous vision of the whole Jesus.

"Thus you see," Father Oshida resumed after the chuckling had subsided, "when John recounts the miracle of the changing of water into wine at the marriage feast at Cana, he sees the water and blood flowing from the side of Jesus on the cross, at one and the same time. Cana, the echo of the *dhyana* of Jesus and Mary, echoes the mystery of water and blood on the cross. In the Cana passage, John wanted to say who Jesus is, who his mystical body is. This conversation of mother and son is full of the mystery of God.

"Mary intervenes, 'They have no wine.' Jesus responds, 'Woman, what concern is that to you and to me? My hour has not yet come'" (John 2:3-4).

"Wedding and crucifixion are one," called out a Trappist monk, awakening to what Father Oshida was saying.

Now I understood too.

Father Oshida nodded, recognizing our moment of suddenly becoming aware of John's pregnant word as event.

> When Jesus calls a female "Woman," it is a sign that a revelation is about to be made. We see that in John's account of the wedding at Cana, and also when he says to the Samaritan woman at the well, "Woman, believe me, the hour is coming when you will worship the Father neither on this mountain nor in Jerusalem. . . . But the hour is coming, and is now here, when the true worshipers will worship the Father in spirit and truth, for the Father seeks such as these to worship him" (John 4:21,23).
>
> After the scribes and Pharisees abandon the woman they say was caught in the very act of adultery and who, they insist, the Law requires should be stoned to death, Jesus speaks to her directly, "Woman, where are they? Has no one condemned you?" (John 8:10). It is an instance unveiling the new law of mercy. Jesus on the Cross addresses his mother as "Woman": "Woman, here is your son," he tells her, meaning the Beloved Disciple, who is to take Mary into his home (John 19:26).
>
> "Do whatever he tells you," Mary says to the servants at Cana (John 2:5). Why does she say that? Because she is the eye in the Hand of God. She is looking into God. She knows that when her son accepts his time, the Hand of God moves. By this miracle, Jesus' first radical fundamental sign, Jesus accepts his time, and accepts the jars of water of suffering people to come.
>
> It is the inception of his mission.
>
> We can say the piercing of Jesus' side occurs approximately around 4:00 o'clock, an hour after his death, which Matthew and Mark tell us is at 3:00. Probably the Cana wedding occurs late in the afternoon too. Why is this important? Because for John, the hours of the passion parallel the hours and days of the life of Jesus. John marks them as his report unfolds.

So at the very beginning of the gospel, when Andrew and another disciple of John the Baptist ask Jesus, "Rabbi, where are you staying?" and Jesus replies, "Come and see," we perceive the depth of the phrase, "It was about four in the afternoon" (John 1:38-39). For John, the hour the Baptist's two disciples follow and stay with Jesus reverberates with the hour blood and water flowed from Christ's side on the Cross. This word "stay" or "remain" is so important to John. At the very end of the gospel, when Jesus tells Peter to follow him, and Peter is worried about leaving John behind, Jesus says to him, "If it is my will that he remain until I come, what is that to you? Follow me!" So the rumor spread among the brothers and sisters that this disciple would not die. Yet Jesus did not say to him that he would not die, but, "If it is my will that he remain until I come, what is that to you?" (John 21:22-23).

John is seized at this point, realizing he is to "remain."

"Where are you staying, Lord?" "Come and see." Four o'clock. Eternal time, not calendar time. John stayed where he was—seized by the Hand of God, beneath the cross, at four o'clock. That is why toward the end of his life he could say nothing but "God is love."

These "four o'clocks" are not mere coincidence. When he writes that others are staying or remaining with Jesus, as he does at the beginning of his gospel, John is seized again. It is his *dhyana*. The whole of life is there. John's whole life. Every word with a contemplative person is contemplative. This is the place John remains. They saw where Christ was staying. "It was about four in the afternoon." John time.

What is "four o'clock"? Some day you will encounter it. John is not just sharing his imaginative perception. He is saying, "I am writing you to go to the place where he is."

Bell, bow, *itadakimasu, gasshō.*

A deeply moved and delighted *zendo* flock adjourned for the night, absorbing what were for most of us "new things" in the Gospel of John—the address "Woman" as revelatory moment, the Virgin Mother Mary as the eye in the Hand of

God, the symmetry of time and "four o'clock," and the gathering kaleidoscope of scene and event.

For myself, who had read so many studies of John and commentaries when as a deacon I was preparing homilies, Oshida's "Word-Event" vision of John was a complete revelation. I never again read the Gospel of John—nor, indeed, Scripture in general and the gospels in particular—in the same ways I had previously: using the Ignatian method (examination of conscience; imagination; personal colloquy), the *lectio divina* way ("dwelling" with the text under the guidance of the Holy Spirit), or the historical-critical approach (the Word of God in its historical and cultural context).

Now instead I always look first through the lens of Father Oshida's kaleidoscope.

Day Five: Thursday

Homily: "The Weight"

At this morning's Eucharist, Father Oshida gathered his reflections on the first four chapters of John under a single rubric, the weight of tears, the Word-Event of the cross. The Mass marked the midpoint of the weeklong *sesshin*, and everyone seemed singularly touched, including Father Oshida. The collective sense was one of moving ever more deeply into the mystery of Jesus the Christ, of being drawn by the Word. Faces looked hushed and expectant; our sitting smoother and more relaxed.

We especially looked forward to hearing and seeing Father's homily.

"Our life of encounter with God," he began, holding up the index finger of both hands to underscore his point, "is precisely like these passages from John: each state, each moment, is one picture. And in one scene other scenes come in. Our life is seen by God in this way. The encounter with the Hand of God that Peter, John, and others experience is always in this way. It is the place where one carries one's own cross. We are always ready to carry someone else's cross or any other cross but our own. But you must accept yours. It is there in carrying your own cross that you discover the Hand of God.

"So, you must discover your cross," he emphasized. "This cross of yours is connected with the cross of others. Jesus is there. Your burden is light."

He signaled the lightness of rising air by exhaling slowly and lifting both hands like an ascending cloud.

> Christ carries it. It is this Hand of God John saw at the cross in the dead Jesus. He saw it after Christ died in the blood and water that poured from his side. In writing John is weeping with the weight he cannot carry. To read the Bible is to feel this weight, to carry this cross with John. We are carrying this cross today. Jesus is saying to us, "Come and see" (John 1:39).

After the Mass, Father Oshida snuffed out the candle and held us in a long silence. The hushed stillness enfolded a hymn to the Blessed Virgin Mary, which he sang in Latin, and then in Japanese, in his distinctive haunting voice. It was *Salve, Regina* ("Hail, Holy Queen"), an anonymous medieval Latin hymn.

> *Salve, Regina, mater misericordiae:*
> *Vita, dulcedo, et spes nostra, salve.*
> *Ad te clamamus, exsules, filii Hevae.*
> *Ad te suspiramus, gementes et flentes*
> *In hac lacrimarum valle.*
> *Eia ergo, Advocata nostra,*
> *Illos tuos misericordes oculos*
> *Ad nos converte.*
> *Et Jesum, benedictum fructum ventris tui,*
> *nobis, post hoc exsilium ostende.*
> *O clemens! O pia!*
> *O dulcis Virgo Maria!*

Hail, holy Queen, Mother of Mercy,
Our life, our sweetness, and our hope.
To thee do we cry, poor banished children of Eve.
To thee do we send up our sighs,
Mourning and weeping in this vale of tears.
Turn then, O most gracious Advocate,
Thine eyes of mercy towards us.
And after this, our exile,
Show unto us the blessed fruit of thy womb, Jesus.
O clement! O loving!
O sweet Virgin Mary!

"Yesterday," he said in an earnest tone of voice, "one of you asked me privately about my personal experience of 'the wind blows wherever it pleases' in the passage from John where Jesus tells Nicodemus, the Pharisee who secretly visits Jesus at night, that he must be born again through water and the Spirit, the wind 'from above.'"

He picked up his Bible and read the passage: "The wind blows wherever it pleases. You hear its sound, but you cannot tell where it comes from or where it is going. So it is with everyone who is born of the Spirit" (John 3:8).

"Allow me to share a few words," he said, referring to his experience of "the wind."

I almost died several times. Once, after the war, I was pulled from the sea, stiff, a hardened body. My lungs were full of water. I was already dead. Someone gave me artificial respiration. It was the beginning of my life. Since then I have approached death again, hemorrhaging from morning to night. Blood was infused by boring into my breastbone.

Death is better than that. My veins were shot. I literally did not move for eight months. Day and night I made myself breathe as though I were not breathing. To use the bedpan, I was barely able to lift my leg.

The doctor stopped all medication. "Please pardon me," he pleaded. "I have to discontinue treating you to save the other patients." There were not enough drugs. War time. I was happy. How frank the doctor is!

But then I thought, "Can I die with the church as it is, leaving it in that state, the friend of rich and authoritative people? I cannot die."

I was feeling something of the mystery of death: an insecurity, but not really the fear of death. The doctor was afraid. He said, "We cannot accept responsibility for your case, so please leave." I got penicillin from a friend. After a year I was cured completely. There was no trace of the illness in my lung.

When I reflect back to the moment when I was thinking "I cannot die," it seems to me there was something in that time, but I was not aware of it.

There was no Roshi around to talk to.

To me, that enigmatic "something" was his evolving mission to renew the Catholic Church in the light of Jesus in the gospels, which was realized in his affirmative response to a divine calling to form with others the Takamori Hermitage community—to make the Catholic Church less a citadel of European Christianity and conventional Western values, and more Japanese. This meant, on the one hand, inculturation and indigenization—assimilating traditional Japanese values and culture and inviting their influence on the evolution of Christian teachings—and, on the other, living radically the Way of Jesus: nonviolence, simplicity, poverty, welcoming all persons, and embracing the other's "Way."

This interior struggle over the mystery of that "something" within that was goading him on became a deep struggle for Father Oshida, to which he alluded as he went on, reflecting on his near-drowning and the surprising discovery of his ego-driven existence.

I went to the monastery in Japan as a novice. Our novice master was a zealous man. We got up at two in the morning two or three times a week, an irregular schedule. I did it. I was not prudent. I again collapsed and was sent to the hospital hemorrhaging. The right lung was already corrupted. The left lung was in trouble. For the first time I felt the fear of death. I felt I had wasted all my life.

At that moment I saw all my past and I remembered, for example, how I would not eat but distributed food door to door. It was my passion: my zealous emotion. It was not by the Holy Spirit. It was my halo. I received an arrow in my chest. I tasted what ego is, arrogance.

Since then, my spiritual life has become a stroll with my hands in my pockets—to get free of the smell of ego It was the beginning of my new life.

Even when I went to the seminary in Ottawa, I was in the same state. The director of the Canadian seminary said, "You are receiving *sapientia* (wisdom) according to theology."[2] It seems to me this gift of wisdom was a two-edged sword, yes, enlightening, but deeply painful as well.

After Oshida's moving homily we somberly bowed together, signaling that it was time to exit the *zendo*. I remarked to the physics teacher behind me, *sotto voce*, "Father Oshida says the Master Teacher of his contemplative prayer, his guru, is his sickness, a sickness that proved to be both physical and spiritual." This teacher was the one who, earlier, had questioned Father Oshida's "logic."

"It seems it is really so," he replied with a sad smile.

Morning Teisho: *"A Voice Crying in the Wilderness"*

It had been a hot, muggy August night and morning. As Father Oshida began his morning *teisho*, a brief shower followed by sunlight breaking through the clouds cleared the air. It felt like a moment of grace, the free and gratuitous gift of God. Everyone's face was shining, including Father Oshida's. Standing before us, he bowed in salutation, straight ahead and to the right, to the light coming through the *zendo* windows.

"I want to turn to another light," he began. "The light of John's *dhyana*, his enlightenment, which we see in his Preface to the Gospel of John. It opens with these lines." He picked up

[2] Father Tarte, Oshida's novice master in Japan, also said he was experiencing *sapientia*, one of the seven gifts of the Holy Spirit.

his Bible, sat down, and read dramatically, his voice rising and falling rhythmically with each line:

> In the beginning was the Word, and the Word was with God, and the Word was God. He was in the beginning with God. All things came into being through him, and without him not one thing came into being. What has come into being in him was life, and the life was the light of all people. The light shines in the darkness, and the darkness did not overtake it (John 1:1-5).

" 'In the beginning *is* the Word,' " he said, ignoring the imperfect tense of the Greek and emphasizing the present. "The word John uses for 'Word' is '*logos*,' Word-Event. Everything happens through it. The beginning is now. John is experiencing this.

"Are you?" he asked, poignantly, looking into our eyes as he peered at each of us in the *zendo*.

"Yes, I'm experiencing it," someone murmured softly from behind me.

"A beginning."

Oshida nodded knowingly. He proceeded, underscoring certain insights as he spoke.

> Ask yourself what is your experience of Christ? Can it be John's? Like the rest of John's Gospel, the Preface is written in light of John's enlightenment, his *dhyana*, his seeing blood and water flow from the dead Christ's side as he hung on the cross. The "In the beginning" verse is a koan. Recall the "Come Holy Spirit" prayer, which says, "And you shall renew the face of the earth."
>
> Actually, it does not mean the world shall be created or renewed. It means, "Come, and every event happens." It too is a koan. Word-Event.
>
> John the Baptist then appears, sent from God, as a witness to the light (John 1:8). What has happened to the Baptist as he calls for repentance and proclaims Christ? He has been split in two and united with God, the Word-Event

realization of the meaning of "purification," *tahara* in He-brew.[3] His words are a true confession expressing the joyous awareness that we are sinners. Yet the priests and Levites are mystified by him. "Is he the Messiah, Elijah returned from the dead, or some resurrected prophet?" they ask.

The Baptist's answer is "No." He is not the Messiah, Elijah, nor a prophet. He declares he is "the voice of one crying out in the wilderness" (John 1:23). Why was John's voice a voice in the desert? Because in the desert the most basic need is expressed and is heard. None of this in the Gospel of John is a description of events. It is not something to understand. The gospel writer is not talking about phenomenon, but *dhyana*, a true calling.

Father Oshida turned and looked at me. "Lucien," he asked, "where have *you* been since yesterday? Be in the place where *you* should be."

I was shocked to be called on. I knew he wasn't asking me about my whereabouts since the previous day, but for a realization of my true self, the Baptist's "voice in the wilderness."

It was a koan, and I was stumped.

Oshida moved on quickly.

> The Baptist says other things that point to the hidden identity of Jesus and are Word-Events echoing his own self-realization. In the same sphere as "Do this in memory of me" are the words, "This was he of whom I said, 'He who comes after me ranks ahead of me because he was before me'" (John 1:15). He is the Beginning where there is *no* Beginning. There is no "Beginning" in the Source, the Hand, the Voice, the Word. "I myself did not know him, but the reason I came baptizing with water was that he might be revealed to Israel" (John 1:31). When John the Baptist sees Jesus walking toward him, he exclaims, "Here is the Lamb of God who takes away the sin of the world!" (John 1:29).

---

[3] In traditional Jewish practice, *tahara* refers to the preparation or purification of the body for its final rest, until the resurrection of the dead.

Suddenly, Father Oshida arose and strutted about the *zendo*, marching as though he were on parade, gracefully weaving his way among the sitters, looking neither left or right, but somehow making his way without hitting anyone or anything, *zafu*, or *zabuton*.

"This is Jesus on parade," he declared as he sat down again, returning to his place in the *zendo*, "and we must feel the weight of the Baptist's testimony."

> We must taste it! John really suffers the hiddenness of Jesus. Always the true identity of the Lamb is hidden. Mary, Jesus' mother, knew Jesus was the Messiah, but she did not know his mission. John "did not know him," but woke up to "he came after me but is before me."
>
> "Lamb of God" is not just an imaginary simile, but the Baptist's deep experience of divine mercy. He heard and saw the Word of God coming from the Hand of God and he translated this mystical experience. The Baptist had the look—he saw the whole.

Father was so moved that his whole countenance changed color, and he unexpectedly began breathing quickly and heavily, as if he were losing his breath. The French yoga teacher was alarmed and she arose to assist him, but he waved her off. After breathing deeply for a spell, he continued. "When John the Evangelist writes, his whole existence is weeping, like John the Baptist." He raised his arms and formed a half-circle to indicate amplitude.

"We too must beg and pray for the faraway vision, or else we waste our lives. Accept every difficulty with gratitude. Your cross is connected with the cross of others. Christ is there. '*Deo gratias.*' Once a mystic lady offered her lung to replace one of mine, removed because of tuberculosis. I said 'no.' Everyone has his cross, his event."

"Our self is unique."

The bishop from Canada spoke up, "Father Oshida," he observed, "for me, when you speak about John the Evangelist and his tears, the pain of personal witness, it makes me think of vocation, of hearing the Voice you spoke about before."

Oshida appeared moved by this bishop who was hearing the Voice. "I am happy for you, glad that you are not simply listening, but hearing," he said.

> What I don't know is what most of you are feeling, whether or not you are religious clergy. You may fear to follow what you hear. For us today, in contrast to the first disciples, a good sign of vocation is, "I can't go!" For the disciples, Jesus' call is clear and unmistakable. "Come and see," he says to Andrew (John 1:39). He gives Simon a new name, "You will be called Cephas," meaning 'the Rock,' a sign of his vocation (John 1:42). He tells Philip, "Follow me" (John 1:43). To Nathanael, Jesus shows his apocalyptic vision, promising "you will see heaven opened and the angels of God ascending and descending upon the Son of Man," meaning the saving power of the Cross (John 1:51).
>
> All these disciples who are called, like John the Baptist and John the Evangelist, must reveal Jesus.

There was a long silence.

I watched Father Oshida's eyes steadily, as he looked around the *zendo*, seeing if others understood what it meant to "be called." I felt many did, as most were seasoned Christians or practiced Buddhists. Others must have wondered.

My own heart ached. I had experienced "I can't go!" once when I received word I had a serious death-threatening illness and refused to accept death, even if it was God's will.

Eventually, like many Christians and Buddhists, in a way I did "go." With a sense of great peace I accepted death should it come. And through our New Covenant Community, we did try to share what we had with the poor.

"And where does Jesus go first?" Oshida suddenly asked, breaking the meditation.

He paused, waiting and waiting for an answer, but as no one said anything, he rang the bell, leaving us hanging. We bowed chanting *"Itadakimasu,"* and parted for the evening meal, feeling called toward some vocation, already known or yet to be conceived.

Evening Teisho: *"We Have the Truth"*

While Grace, the mother of five, tiptoed about the *zendo*, taking her turn to light the candles, Father Oshida sat and rang the bell, calling us together for this evening's *teisho*. Once we had found our places, some of us noticed he was smiling, achingly.

"One day," he recalled, "the representative of our order asked me, 'Do you believe the Dominican Order can exist as it is in the Orient?' His own answer was that it could not. 'But,' he said, 'let's not tell those who haven't made their vows yet!' "

Everyone in the *zendo* laughed aloud, then immediately fell silent.

Father Oshida was not laughing. The hypocrisy of a brother Dominican, even though intended in jest, must have tasted painfully bitter to him. As I already mentioned, I had accompanied him as he went around New England visiting fellow Dominican sisters and priests. In conversations and talks his face would shine. Obviously, he loved being a Dominican.

> We judge the institutional church, not because it is an institution, but because it does not have the eye that God has given us. The criteria of the institutional church are the laws it has made. Having this God-given eye, let us carry the sub-currents of the Mystical Body, the need of the little ones, of the Holy Innocents carrying this mystery. That is our only plan. The church can exist even in Asia, but never in its present form—an institutional, rational church of Pharisees.
>
> The Japanese know in their blood what religion is. The Catholic Church is not a box of chocolates or a business. Give up the church's money and send it back to Africa and other economically underdeveloped areas from which it came.

Some of the retreatants—laity, monks, sisters, priests—squirmed a little on their cushions upon hearing Oshida's radical stance, even though they may have agreed with him. Others were thrilled, as was I. It was like listening to Jesus among the cynics, scribes, and those Pharisees who were his enemies. Whatever our interior response might be, Oshida persisted with his critique. "Now is the time to sow the seed," he insisted, "to have people taste Jesus."

> As in the time of Jesus, this happens among suffering people, people who are in agony. It is the time of exodus for the church. Today the seminary has everything. Christ is not necessary anymore. But what is important is not numbers but quality and depth. This exodus is connected with the destiny of humanity. There is the threat of the annihilation of humanity, not just materially, but the annihilation of the mystery of the Incarnation. It is the challenge of the devil.
>
> I want to make a retreat with Japanese bishops, but there is no occasion. Everyone feels the problem but they do not listen to the Voice of God. The Catholic Church today has become an institution that kills the spirit. Some Catholic sisters came to Takamori and laughed when they were asked to clean out the toilets. They would not do it. A Buddhist monk cleaned up after them. It is a shame. The Buddhist monks take care of their own misfits and outcasts. The Catholic Church sends theirs to us at Takamori. They think we are an institution. They send their misfits to us. They do not take care of them themselves.

Father Oshida scowled.

He went on to speak about the liturgy of the Mass.

> What I suffer most is the display of words. We make noises. It is what pains me the most in the life of the church. When Jesus was in the garden of Gethsemane, did he bring a presider's chair? When Abraham and Jesus prayed, they bowed down and prostrated themselves. Remember Adam and Eve. No flush. Toilet paper wrecks manure and wastes

money. So don't think the flush is a sign of civilization. I
suggest that you take away these things—altars and what-
not—and then you will begin to taste Jesus.

For several years at Takamori I suffered the altar. Suddenly I heard the Voice, "Take away the altar." And I sat
zazen like the others. Jesus said, "Yes, it is your way of doing
this mystery here." The altar smelled of all this structure,
all the traditions of *"gloria Romana."* Recently, there was an
ordination at my place. The bishop said: "What, Takamori
is so far away and I cannot sit on a cushion on the floor!
Please prepare a chair for me." We had a little elevated altar
and a chair. But it is not for us. We should be naked at the
liturgy as on the cross.

Late that night I found myself meditating on Father Oshida's
critique of the institutional Western or European Catholic
Church. His censure rang in my ears loud and clear. I thought
about how I as a Catholic had so often yearned for this nakedness, this return to radical simplicity and the universal appeal
of the gospel but had not found it. Thus, friends and my wife
and I, while remaining keen to continue practicing our Catholic
faith—weekly Mass, sacramental life, and service to the church
and the poor—had started the New Covenant Community.

My desire for nakedness and simplicity was encouraged by
Vatican II's call for *aggiornamento*, renewal through the return
to the sources of the Catholic faith and adaption to the changed
conditions of the age. These were the underlying guidelines
of our New Covenant Community as we sought to embody
the teaching and spirit of Vatican II.

In Father Oshida I had found a remarkable and inspiring
expression of inculturation, the council's teaching that the
Catholic faith must incorporate the cultures of all who receive
the gospel, and must "think, speak, and ritualize according to
the local cultural pattern."[4] This is what Father Oshida did at

---

[4] Anscar Chupungco, *Cultural Adaptation of the Liturgy* (Mahwah, NJ:
Paulist Press, 1982), 30. See also Peter Schineller, *A Handbook on Inculturation*
(Mahwah, NJ: Paulist Press, 1990).

Takamori and in his celebration of the Eucharist. I suspect that he was conscious of Vatican II, the dates of which—from 1963 to 1965—coincided with the founding of Takamori Soan in 1964 and that he was familiar with the theology of inculturation. I do not think, however, that he was explicitly intending to implement the teachings of Vatican II or the theology of inculturation with his founding of Takamori. Rather, he was simply being himself, a Japanese Buddhist-Christian with the "God-given eye," swimming in the "sub-currents of the Mystical Body."

As I mulled over Father Oshida's words, I realized that there was within me a deep interior attraction to Japanese aesthetics, *wabi-sabi*, the appeal to the eye of beauty that is imperfect, transient, and incomplete. Thus, my delight in Takamori's thatched-roof huts was more intense than my admiration of the vaults and stained-glass windows of European cathedrals.

At Takamori I found my ideal incarnated.

Father Oshida stood up and stretched. He was tired after a long day reflecting on the Gospel of John, yet he was moved to share just one more thing—the gospel writer's narrative of the singular moment Jesus suddenly appears in Jerusalem for the first time, and the shocking act with which he begins his active ministry—the cleansing of the temple (John 2:13-25). Situating this event at the beginning of Jesus' public life is peculiar to John and stands in strong contrast to its placement in the three Synoptic Gospels, where the cleansing takes place at the end of Jesus' career.

After loosening up his back and massaging his legs and arms, he resumed sitting.

"Following his call to his first disciples and performing his first sign at the wedding at Cana in Galilee," Oshida reminded us, "Jesus goes up to Jerusalem since the Passover is near."

He begins the work of the New Horizon hinted at in Galilee.
His first act is the driving out of the money changers. I

meditated on this passage of the cleansing of the temple for twenty years before I understood it.

Why does John place it where he does, at the beginning of Jesus' career, instead of towards the end, as in the Synoptics?

John felt the need of purifying the scene—the temple, Jerusalem—the place where major events were to take place. His was a purging of Word-Idea, of human arrogance, the hidden face that is so concealed in us.

John was crying within himself, "The hour has come" (John 12:23). He was obliged to perform this action.

As for you, think about your time, your life. Don't dwell in general upon your personal sanctification or ponder the spiritual life in a logical way. Such reflection is a trick of the devil. The hour has come to rid the church and schools of tricks. Feel everything with your time like John does. The uniqueness of this moment. The hidden face. This hour is not meant for general enlightenment. It is not a gymnasium you enter to practice spiritual exercises. It is the sense of Zen. It is the mystery of faith. *Kairos.*

Oshida reached for the bell to end the evening, when Russell, a young man from Canada, interrupted him, indicating he wanted to ask something. He had come all the way from Vancouver, British Columbia, where he worked in an art gallery. Despite being spent, Oshida held his hands palms up and raised his forearms, inviting the young man to speak.

"Father Oshida" he appealed, "I have been wondering about the cleansing of the temple for a long time. Not so much about where it appears in John's gospel, but how powerful and shocking it is. You say Jesus 'was obliged to perform this action.' Why? What do you mean by 'the hidden face' that you see as the real target of the scourging of the money changers?"

Father Oshida suddenly looked down wearily, his face drawn and conflicted. He nodded, taking in the question, and rang the bell.

Bell, bow, *itadakimasu, gasshō.*

Day Six: Friday

We gathered in the *zendo*, found our places, bowed, and sat down. I could see that most of us were familiar with the Zen meditation procedure by now. There were fewer groans than earlier in the week but sitting with our legs crossed was still painful for most of us. After a hot, sultry August night, the wide-open windows brought a welcome breath of fresh cool air into the *zendo* along with the bright morning light.

This was day six of our *sesshin*. We assembled quietly, anticipating another beautiful morning Eucharist. Always there were surprises, whether it was during the Mass itself or the homily.

Father Oshida entered the *zendo* and bowed his head solemnly, lower and more slowly than usual. I wondered whether he was carrying some weight on his heart from the night before. He sat immobile for several long minutes.

Looking up I saw anguish in his face. What was troubling him? Was it still the Catholic Church in Japan and in the West, as it was last night?

Homily: "The Hidden Face"

"Last evening I felt uncomfortable," Father Oshida began, sitting with his legs crossed. He raised both hands and extended his arms, inviting our full attention.

"Something kept me awake all night long. I had the impression I was misunderstood when talking about Jesus' cleansing of the temple, about our hidden face and human arrogance."

To my mind, Oshida had been referring to the shadow or dark side of ourselves, the side we would prefer not to see or acknowledge nor want others to see, though they do. It is the side Jesus sees in the Jewish authorities and the money changers. His furious reaction is the cleansing of the temple. But for Oshida himself there apparently was a deeper personal significance on which he wished to elaborate.

He stood up, and looked around the *zendo*, scrutinizing each sitter.

> In the gospel this face appears, the face of arrogance. When the Jews ask Jesus, "We are descendants of Abraham and have never been slaves to anyone. What do you mean by saying, 'You will be made free'?" (John 8:33), he delivers his last punch. Jesus does not retire. He pushes to the extreme. His words are strong.
>
> "You are from your father the devil, and you choose to do your father's desires" (John 8:44). The devil is not rooted in bare reality. He brings out his own things from his belly. The devil is not rooted. He works at the phenomenal level.

Paraphrasing, Oshida proceeded, "You, the Jewish authorities, do the same thing. You and the devil believe this belly is absolute because you are not rooted in the bare reality. You leaders of the Jewish people, the Chosen People—now we know—you are possessed by the devil."

"If war begins, it is by that hidden face, not by reasoning. Reasoning comes later. This is why Jesus speaks of 'the narrow gate.' " He picked up his well-worn black leather English Bible from the coffee table beside him, and quietly and solemnly read a short paragraph, his face distorted as though torn by a wound. "Enter through the narrow gate; for the gate is wide and the road is easy that leads to destruction, and there are many who take it. For the gate is narrow and the road is hard that leads to life, and there are few who find it "(Matt 7:13-14).

"The condemnation of any other culture reveals the attitude of the hidden face, collective arrogance," he stated succinctly.

> Most Japanese have the hidden face of being anti-Chinese, and Chinese often have the hidden face of being anti-Japanese. This is as hidden as it is personal. Everywhere I go in the world, I do not feel a stranger. How it is I don't know. But when I hear a word of insult against an Arab spoken by a Jew, I cannot sleep. If there is a word against

myself or my Japanese culture, I should be very happy. If you throw stones at me, I shall sing for joy. I shall go with Jesus.

But if I myself feel anti-Chinese or sense your hidden face, I cannot sleep. It affects me. All races have it. All of us share this arrogance of the hidden face, of being certain we are right and the other is wrong. I hope everyone here honors the real mystical body, beyond all cultures, full of respect for each culture, a simple feeling of being the friend and brother of Jesus. Without that we have no assurance of the survival of humanity today.

I think Father Oshida may have detected some anti-Japanese prejudice among us, perhaps in two or three retreat participants, but I was uncertain. What was clear was his own painful admittance of the reality of racism in Japan, of being anti-Chinese and anti-Korean.

Most poignantly, he touched on that reality in himself. It was an incredible moment of vulnerable truth.[5]

Oshida looked up, tears in his eyes.

"If you see a baby dying on the street you will see Jesus. If you see bones after an atomic bomb blast, they are no longer bones. You will see Jesus. It is the devil who made us do that work," he said, meaning the United States dropping A-bombs on Hiroshima and Nagasaki.

"I am sure John weeps as he writes down the lines describing the cleansing of the temple."

Many of us were weeping as well, mindful of our hidden face of bigotry.

I thought of my youthful arrogance, my making fun of a boy in elementary school who was somehow "different"—skinny, tall, and stooped over, and whose red hair stuck out like a rooster comb down the middle of his head—and my failure to stand up for a gay man who lived with my family

---

[5] I am grateful to Russell Keziere, *sesshin* participant, for this insight regarding Father Oshida's confession of his hidden face.

when I was in high school, when my father's business friends made fun of him.

And what about now? Dare I confess in public? No, I dare not.

But I can weep generously inside.

After morning Mass, I walked slowly on the trail through the Mary House woods, which led to St. Joseph's Abbey that lay atop the hills above. I had built the trail years before and did periodic clean-ups—once with the help of my Soto Zen friend, Issho Fujita, clearing brush and stones from the path, so that students and retreatants could use it to go from Mary House to the abbey instead of walking on the dangerous highway that cut through the valley.

Today, calling to mind the Remembrance Wood at Takamori, dedicated to those who died or were killed by the Japanese military during World War II and preceding eras, I pray for the Holy Innocents destroyed by the Hidden Face in America—our Hiroshima and Nagasaki: atomic bombs, abortion, genocide of native peoples, enslavement of African Americans, which began in 1619 with the arrival of the first boatload of Africans in Virginia, and centuries of individual Catholics participating in the slave trade and the Catholic Church's complicity in racism. How painful it is to think of ourselves as the enslaving and genocidal nation we have been.

Morning Teisho: *"The New Horizon"*

"Where did Jesus go first?" Father Oshida asked playfully, sitting on his *zafu*, returning to the question he asked in yesterday's morning *teisho*. He raised one hand flat over his eyebrows, like a cowboy or a boy scout shielding his eyes from the sunlight, as if he were scouring the *zendo* for signs of life.

"To Galilee," he declared heartily wearing an impish smile, not waiting for a response. "Jesus himself tells us that he is 'sent' by the Father on his divine mission (John 4:34). But why Galilee? Nathanael knows Jesus is from Nazareth in Galilee

and exclaims, 'Can anything good come out of Nazareth?' "
(John 1:46).

"Every village in Israel is mentioned in the Torah, has a
tradition of being touched by the Hand of God, except Nazareth. It is a lowly place, the place of the poor. They did not have
a library," Oshida commented, laconically.

He stood up and beckoned to my wife's and my dear friend
and our soulmate, Anne Kusmin Martens, a graphic artist and
book designer, to come with him. A Catholic convert and Jew
whose Judaism became a dwelling place for Christ, Anne ema-
nated a holy presence and unity of being, mirroring Father
Oshida's mystical oneness as Buddhist Zen master and Catholic
priest. All eyes were on the two as they walked over to the Mary
House library alcove a few feet away, where Father Oshida
motioned for Anne to sit on the library stool and "check out"
the pile of books he proceeded to scoop from the shelves.

He carefully thumbed through one hefty volume she se-
lected and handed him, feigning intense interest in the title
which he read aloud in a booming voice: *"A Comparative Study
of the Religions of the World."*

Oshida looked astonished and exclaimed in Japanese, *"Ah,
so desu!"* as if to say "Here's what I have been talking about!"
He put down the volume after pretending to peruse its con-
tents ever so slowly.

"Nathanael's questioning whether anything good can come
from Nazareth can't be answered in an encyclopedia!"

We laughed in agreement.

"When Nathanael meets Jesus in Galilee," Oshida went on,
"and Jesus says he knows him because he saw him sitting
under a fig-tree, Nathanael immediately proclaims who Jesus
is: 'Rabbi, you are the Son of God! You are the King of Israel!'
(John 1:49)."

Obviously, it seemed to me this was an instance of Word-
Event, not Word-Idea.

Father Oshida escorted his "librarian" back to her *zafu*,
while everyone clapped. We all knew he had only pretended

to find a comparative religions encyclopedia. He sat for a long span of time, then stretched his legs and stood up.

> Galilee is the New Horizon. Galilee is key. The hidden Jesus appears there. Again, as I mentioned before, it is the place where he goes on parade—the Baptist proclaiming and Cana revealing. Galilee is the location of his teaching by the sea. At the Last Supper, Jesus tells his disciples that after his resurrection, he will go before them to Galilee (Matt 26:32). They will find the resurrected Jesus in Galilee (Matt 28:7,10; Mark 14:28; 16:7). He appears to them at the shore of the Sea of Galilee (John 21:1-23). For Jesus, the will of God is in Galilee.
>
> Jesus is not just talking about a phenomenon, about a place. The will of God appears where Jesus is, where you are, in Galilee. The New Horizon.
>
> In all these episodes, it is the New Horizon. Jesus, the observer, sees the Father act within him, and he acts. He cannot do otherwise. The New Horizon is a time of fear and wonder, of transfiguration, walking on water, multiplying loaves, and eating the body and blood of Jesus. The New Horizon always holds Jesus' Pasch, his Passover and deliverance. He is ever looking forward.
>
> Jesus is the event of God.

Oshida paused, reflecting. Then he walked down the middle of the *zendo* to an open window that faced southeast and opened his arms to absorb the rising morning sun flooding the room full of sitters.

Turning around and facing us, he proclaimed, "Now is the time of the New Horizon of Spirit and truth. The New Horizon is not Jewish, not Christian, not Buddhist."

When Father Oshida returned to his *zafu*, Janet Ward, the young Catholic Worker from New York, flung up her hand.

"Was Nicodemus the Pharisee part of the New Horizon?" she asked earnestly, a puzzled look on her face. "Would I recognize the New Horizon?"

Oshida nodded affirmatively to both questions. Nicodemus was indeed part of the New Horizon. And as a Catholic Worker she knew the New Horizon by heart.

Knowing her, I was well aware this was true. She lived for the poor.

Father Oshida elaborated on Nicodemus whom he had mentioned earlier. Nicodemus's awareness of Jesus' prophetic spirit was dangerous for him, a threat to others. He came "at night" to visit Jesus. It was a risk for him to come to see Jesus.

The conversation between Jesus and Nicodemus is a revelation of the essentials of the cross, the "things of heaven." Jesus wishes to jolt Nicodemus, and so he speaks of the "Son of Man" who has gone up to and come down from heaven and who must be "lifted up" so believers may have eternal life. He also speaks of the "only Son of God," a phrase of apposite voltage, who is to save the world (John 3:14-18).

> Nicodemus has some intimation of Jesus. He tells him, "Rabbi, we know that you are a teacher who has come from God; for no one can do these signs that you do apart from the presence of God" (John 3:2).
>
> This is a passage where we should question the translation: "Do these signs that you are doing." It means no one could perform the works you do, that is create from nothing. But Nicodemus cannot understand Jesus' response: he must be "born again" (John 3:3). He thinks it means rebirth. How can an old man like him return to his mother's womb and "be born again"? Nicodemus wonders aloud.

"Of course," a young man called out with a smile, "Old Nick is kidding—tongue in cheek." The young man was a Zen disciple dressed in a formal kimono, a *kesa* or surplice robe, and at his feet were a pair of flat, thonged sandals (*zori*), made of rice-straw.

"His question is not a joke," Oshida flashed back. "Flesh is Woman. Flesh is full of respect. The womb is the place of vocation (Jer 1:5; Isa 49:1), of *dabar*, of Word-Event, not just a place of conception. Nicodemus knows a prophet is called from the womb of his mother. Jesus elaborates solemnly, 'Very truly, I tell you, no one can enter the kingdom of God without being born of water and Spirit'" (John 3:5).

The student stood up and bowed, now understanding clearly.

"Vocation leads to spiritual rebirth," he murmured, "something like that of the young boy in the famous Chinese and Japanese Ox Herder Tale, reunited with his lost ox, enlightened."[6]

Oshida smiled mischievously. "The foolish church thinks this shows the Catholic Church existed already, that 'water and the Spirit' is about baptism.

"Nicodemus, 'the teacher of Israel' cannot grasp how he is to be born of the Spirit and be like the wind, blowing about where it will. 'The wind blows where it chooses, and you hear the sound of it, but you do not know where it comes from or where it goes. So it is with everyone who is born of the Spirit'" (John 3:8).

"Jesus asks, 'If I have told you about earthly things and you do not believe, how can you believe if I tell you about heavenly things?'" (John 3:12).

Oshida then went on.

> "Earthly things" are the things of the earth. Jewish history. Jewish tradition. Things you already know. To become a saint is a thing of the earth. "Heavenly things" means crucifixion and resurrection. Every sign or miracle is a sign of the sign, that is, the cross. It is there that the Hand of God seizes man.
>
> In this encounter, John saw the Hand of the Father clearly. It echoes his experience at the foot of the cross when Christ

---

[6] See William Johnston's explication of the Ox Herder Tale in Lucien Miller, "Wisdom's Flowering Cherry Tree: The Charismatic Zen of William Johnston, SJ," *Dilatato Corde* 11, no. 2 (2021). The essay also appears in *Buddhist-Christian Studies*, vol. 42 (2022) with the title "Wisdom's Flowering Cherry: William Johnston's Charismatic Zen."

expired, breathing out his Spirit, the origin of Pentecost.[7]
"*Ruah*"—breath—*pneuma* and water poured out. Water is
life. Don't take it casually. In Genesis, we read that the Spirit
hovered over the water. This is the condition of being, the
fundamental structure of the mystery of being, Spirit and
water.

Jewish people experienced the Spirit in the water—water
in Noah's story of the flood, the exodus and crossing the
Red Sea, the water God caused to spring from a rock in the
desert, the healing at the pool of Siloam. Spirit and water.
The Hand of God. Once I awoke from a dream and thought
of the mystery of the cross. "The things of heaven." What
does it mean to us? Our personal sanctification? No. That
is "things of the earth." What does it mean, "the things of
heaven"?

The cross. You cannot see the sign of the cross unless you
are reborn.

Suddenly, Father Oshida surprised us, drawing a parallel
to Thomas Merton.

"For Thomas Merton, living the New Horizon spelled his
death. Probably Thomas Merton was killed," he declared.
Why?

Because he said 'yes for yes' like the man in the gospel (Matt
5:37). Merton was the center of the Peace Movement. The
desert of America is a desert, not for the hermit, but for
Satan. Merton was an obstacle. He died materially. Was it
only a human event? If we do not carry his death within
us, we are not Christian. We can forget it if we think it is
only a matter of consciousness, one of the "things of earth."

[7] Ancient Catholic tradition teaches that the church originates in the blood
and water pouring from Christ's side. "From the time of Tertullian [c. 160
AD–c. 225] onwards . . . the Fathers of the church and the early Christian
writers have been unanimous in seeing this as a prophetic announcement of
the wedding between Christ, the new Adam, and the church, the new Eve,
when, from the pierced side of Jesus fallen into the deep sleep of death came
water and blood, the sacraments, baptism and the Eucharist, which build up
the church: the marriage of the Cross and the marriage of the Lamb!" Yves
Congar, *I Believe in the Holy Spirit*, vol. 2 (New York: Seabury, 1983), 56–57.

The stillness in the *zendo* deepened. Practically everyone had read Merton or heard of him. Most knew he had died and were shocked to hear that Oshida thought he had been killed. Oshida, *in memoriam* for Merton, as it were, ceased speaking.

During the long interval, I thought it curious that Father asserted Merton was murdered, mentioning mysterious things, like unidentified footsteps outside the window of the room where he was electrocuted in Thailand. I had heard this speculation before but didn't think to question Oshida about it. Today there is much specious guessing and theorizing, but so far as I know, no definitive evidence to credit this rumor.

What seems clear to me judging from Merton's writings is that his death by electric shock was foretold. The "smell of burnt flesh" and the burnt gash discovered on his dead body hark back to the prophetic end of his first book, his autobiography, *Seven Storey Mountain*, published twenty years before he died, wherein God foretells Merton's death:

> Everything that touches you shall burn you . . . Everything that can be desired will sear you, and brand you with a cautery . . . You will be praised, and it will be like burning at the stake . . . You shall die in Me and find all things in My mercy which has created you for this end . . . That you may become the brother of God and learn to know the Christ of the burnt men.[8]

"Merton was one of Christ's burnt men," I blurted out loud, in effect ending the long silence. I couldn't help myself, suddenly realizing that in Oshida's mind, Galilee, Merton, sudden death and resurrection, Pharisee and Gentile, were viewed from the perspective of the New Horizon to which Jesus alluded

---

[8] Thomas Merton, *The Seven Storey Mountain* (New York: Harcourt, Brace, 1948), 62; Michael Mott, *The Seven Mountains of Thomas Merton* (Boston: Houghton Mifflin, 1984), 464–65. In *Wisdom of the Desert* (New York: New Directions, 1970), Merton recalls the story of an elder monk of the Egyptian desert who tells an aspiring novice: "Why not be totally changed into fire?" (50, passage 72).

when he said to his disciples, "But after I am raised up, I will go ahead of you to Galilee" (Matt 26:32), the place of the New Horizon, where he would meet his disciples again, after his death and resurrection.

My sitting place was but a few feet from Father Oshida's. He nodded, welcoming Merton as burnt man, remembering well the passage from Merton's autobiography.

Bell, bow, *itadakimasu, gasshō.*

Evening Teisho: "The New Horizon"

A few minutes before the *teisho* began I was sitting on my cushion, relaxed, my legs straight out before me, when I noticed one of the retreatants, a newly ordained parish priest, came into the *zendo* bearing an armload of extra candles and began lighting them at various stations within the room, his face suffused with a soft light. He was smitten, thrilled by his discovery of *zazen* and his encounter with Father Oshida, and had decided to incorporate sitting meditation before offering his daily Mass.

Father Oshida settled onto his *zafu* and rang the bell, eager to set his boat in the water and embark, one last time. Everyone, including Father Oshida, looked triumphant, faces and *zendo* radiantly peaceful, like the priest bathed in the additional candlelight. After the *sesshin* he disclosed to me that lighting the candles was an act of love and thanksgiving.

Following the sitting period Father Oshida gave his final *teisho*, returning to the New Horizon, touching on Nicodemus, and elaborating on the woman at the well. He regretted that he would be unable to speak about the rest of John's gospel, especially the passion of Jesus. There simply was not enough time.

Thus far we had gathered that the New Horizon was Galilee in both the literal and figurative sense, a lowly place of the poor where God's will is manifested in Jesus and he is recognized as the Son of God. Galilee is the setting where the hidden

Jesus and the mystery of the cross are revealed. It is Word-Event and being born again. Now Oshida turned to Samaria as also being the New Horizon.

"In these events," Oshida began—"Nicodemus at night, the woman at the well—we discern the evolution of John's writing. It is like the music of Bach repeating the same theme, weaving variations together so beautifully, or, to use a visual image, like a series of slides, one atop the other in a breadth and unity of vision."

> Everything that happens around Jesus carries echoes of the mystery of Jesus because he is Jesus. Each is the event of God. It is the time of the New Horizon. Always we see Jesus responding to the present, to his time, moved by the Hand of God.
>
> At Jacob's Well, in the encounter with the Samaritan woman, he recognizes his hour.
>
> "It was about noon," John tells us, connecting this moment to the time of the Crucifixion. "Give me a drink," he says to her (John 4:6f.). That is, let me drink your waters, your pain, your agony. He is open to the pains of others and takes them into himself. "Who touched me?" he asks, when a woman afflicted with hemorrhages for twelve years pressed lightly on the tassel of his cloak (Luke 8:45). When Jesus received suffering of others, healing took place. God's Hand heals through Jesus.

Oshida unexpectedly halted. His face suddenly turned dark and his eyes glimmered with tears.

"I knew my sin when I refused to receive my mother's suffering," he confessed, pivoting on his *zafu*. "When she was sick and dying, I did not go home to visit her. I was being obedient to my vocation of aloneness. I was a sinner."

Several of us sunk down, feeling the sadness of Father's "confession." It must have been a black time when he left his mother to die alone.

"Give me a drink," he proceeded, quoting Jesus' words to the Samaritan woman at the well (John 4:7).

Carry this word of Jesus until you encounter what it is. Someday God will reveal to you what this water was that Jesus desired.

Why does the Samaritan woman appear here? In reading the Bible, always seek the vision in which the author was obliged to write. Here in John, first there is the revelation of who Jesus Christ is—to a Jewish leader, Nicodemus. Later, he is revealed to the Samaritan woman.

This means the New Horizon has broadened to include Samaria, a rejected hated place. His disciples are amazed to find him talking to a woman (John 4:27). Jews regarded Samaritan women as ritually impure, and therefore Jews were forbidden to drink from any vessel they had handled.[9]

Jesus is tired. It is noon, twelve o'clock, a time connected with the hour of his dying. His request to the Samaritan woman, "Give me a drink" is echoed by his words from the cross, "I am thirsty" (John 19:28). Jesus sees himself on the cross. The presence of the woman of Samaria parallels the women at the cross. Water in the desert context is life. The water from his side is the eternal water. John tasted this thirst of Jesus to the last.

In the end he concluded, "God is love" (1 John 4:8).

"See how far the word of God is from our consciousness, from our word," Oshida remarked sweepingly, checking our faces to see if we grasped what he was saying.

The Samaritan woman says to Jesus she knows the Messiah is coming. But this is a matter beyond consciousness. "But the hour is coming, and is now here, when the true worshipers will worship the Father in spirit and truth, for the Father seeks such as these to worship him" (John 4:23). He reveals to her what he did not reveal to Nicodemus. "I am he, the one who is speaking to you," he tells her (John 4:26).

Jesus is looking at his time, not just the physical historical time, but his mystical body placed in his time. When the disciples return from town with food and invite him to eat, he informs them his food is not of this world. "I have food

---

[9] New American Bible, John 4:9 fn.

to eat that you do not know about. . . . My food is to do the will of him who sent me and to complete his work" (John 4:32, 34).

"I am hungry for this food," Oshida said, rubbing his stomach as he sat.

His mood lightened, his eyes glimmered and he teased us.

He stood up pointing one last time to his "diabolical" pie-chart of "Spheres of the Word," and to the word he suddenly wrote in large letters at its base: "Joy," reminding us of the Unborn Sphere and the depths where lies true joy. Then he went on.

"Joy is not something to explain but to experience," he exclaimed.

> Someone I knew who was suffering from despair happened one day to visit a woman who was smiling. Visiting her made him feel that his despair was a vanity. People like this woman reveal *kavod*, the burden of the weight of being, the plenitude of capacity, the plenitude of divine life, and enable others to feel lighter and transcend misery. They are in the Hand of God.
>
> If a priest gives a sermon and people clap their hands and come up to him after Mass saying, "Father, that was a good sermon," he is pleased. This means that his sermon was not really good. It did not really attach itself to the souls of the people. If it did believers would go before the tabernacle after Mass, forgetting the preacher.
>
> If this happened, a real preacher would say, "What a joy!"
>
> The Hebrew word, *kavod*, is the weight of being, the fullness of honor and righteousness revealed in each person. To experience it, we must become the Suffering Servant. There was a joy in Jesus carrying the cross to Calvary. It is Jesus on the cross who reveals *kavod*. It springs out from the Hand of God.
>
> "He must become greater; I must become less" (John 3:30). And it is my joy! We see the extreme example of this joy in John the Baptist proclaiming Jesus and in Mary singing the Magnificat. "My soul magnifies the LORD, and my spirit rejoices in God my Savior" (Luke 1:46-47).
>
> So we must enter into her womb to be reborn.

There was a long pause before he rang the closing bell. His face shone with his beatific smile, brows raised like quarter moons over his half-shut eyes, his lips parted in a distinctive Cheshire cat grin.

After the final bell and as everyone was milling about and talking, I felt myself overcome with joy. I held my hands up before me, palms up, and looked at them with the wonder of being human. I called out, inviting everyone in the *zendo* to do the same and share my awe and delight. Some sat down and joined me. Others danced or sang or just smiled.

Still others were near tears.

"*Itadakimasu*," we chanted in unison, again and again and again.

A final bell rang out from somewhere in the *zendo*. Someone was trying their hand at ringing out joy.

Day Seven: Saturday Morning

Morning Homily: "Stars on the Cross"

This morning was our last Eucharist together, and in a very brief closing homily Father Oshida shared his final thoughts. He waited until we had all settled down on our *zafu*, then walked over to his blackboard and thoroughly erased his "diabolical" graph of a triangle. He then returned to his place and sat down once again in the lotus position.

"Jesus in the Garden of Gethsemane is essential Zen," he stated simply, referring to the agony Jesus experienced before his arrest and crucifixion, leaving us to guess and interpret his meaning.

It was as though he were giving a last word on what our future practice might be without explaining his meaning. My sense was Gethsemane could be our koan, if you will, our place of meditation, our prayer. Others surely felt the same or something similar, but we did not talk about what was "essential Zen." Already we had tasted so much.

There was a long silence during which he contemplated the *sesshin* participants sitting on their cushions before him in the *zendo*, gazing fondly at each face, one last time. Then he got up and went about the room exchanging greetings and farewells with everyone, somehow remembering something unique about each.

When it was my turn, he bowed and chortled: "Next time I land and get off the plane and you come to pick me up, I won't think 'Lucien' is someone else!"

"*Domo arigato goziamasu!*" I cried in reply.

Returning to his cushion, he continued his homily.

"How do you know the risen Christ?" he suddenly asked enigmatically, looking deeply into the eyes of each one of us. We waited a good while in silence for his answer.

"When you experience helplessness, forgiveness, and freedom. Like a vulnerable bug on its back—flailing its legs in powerlessness. Eventually the bug is set aright—but not by its own power alone—then flies away, free to be itself.

"People who sit together will always be together," he concluded. "Wherever you are, whatever you do, you will be sitting with one another as we have been this week. As we are now. As we always will be."

"Each one of us is a star born of the cross from far away," he concluded with a bow, slowly exiting the *zendo*.

We bowed with palms pressed together one last time, chanting "*Itadakimasu*" with all our hearts one last time.

Farewell

Lunch and Parting

We fetched our lunches from the kitchen. Some remained there to thank Sister Cathy and Sister Jane who had done all the cooking. Others carried their plates to the *zendo*, preferring to eat alone and in silent gratitude. I joined a small group at the dining room table—Sister Jane, who had sprained her ankle at the first sitting; the athletic looking Zen student in his formal kimono, surplice, and zori sandals; Bishop Bill (not his real name) from Newfoundland; Janet, the Catholic worker; our "librarian," Anne, who had pretended to help Father Oshida find a book on world religions; the Jewish couple, now to our mutual delight holding their new baby girl Davina (Adored) with a hint of blond hair; and Father Joseph Chu-Cong, the Trappist abbey's novice master who was Vietnamese.

Bishop Bill, dressed in jeans and a sweatshirt with a "Forgive" logo on the front, spoke first.

> What will stay with me after this retreat and I return to Canada is the word "fire." All through this week, Jesus' words at our first Mass kept ringing in my head: "I have come to bring fire on the earth, and how I wish it were already kindled!" (Luke 12:49). I came because I needed a break and was curious about this Japanese Dominican Buddhist I had heard so much about. Things are very troubling in my diocese. I had become weary, almost without hope. Now I am on fire to follow the gospel of Jesus, to serve his people. Father Oshida is infectious. Listening to him is like catching on fire, catching the disease of love.

We nodded in recognition in one way or another similarly touched by Father's ardor.

"I have discovered something utterly new for me," said the Zen disciple, his eyebrows raised in astonishment, his face shining. "I never dreamed there was someone like Father Oshida in the Roman Catholic Church. He interiorized Catholic-Zen for me. In his Mass and *teisho*, he showed me Jesus. I am not saying that now, somehow, I am 'Catholic.' But I am now more open." He laughed out loud. "Ha! I hesitated about coming because I didn't want my Zen practice to be tainted or mixed up with Christian stuff. Now, I've tasted Jesus through Zen."

"Ha!" echoed Janet Ward, with a smile to the Zen student sitting next to her, her bright eyes gleaming with her own reverse awakening to Zen through Jesus. "After this week New York and the Catholic Worker will never be the same again! Like Bishop Bill, I feel on fire too. Wait until I tell Dorothy Day. I feel illuminated, challenged, wondering what on earth could be next. It has been a week of sheer grace, the gift of the Holy Spirit."

Sister Jane shared a story, as we knew she would.

"Just before this retreat, I took Father Oshida to see a ramshackle tenement in Springfield," she said.

> My community of Saint Joseph Sisters has been thinking about finding a home for the poor in a shockingly run-down area of town. A halfway house that could provide shelter, maybe food, but above all services that would help people get on their feet, especially women and children who have nowhere to go. Father and I toured the old building together. When he got to the fourth floor, he pointed to a tree that was growing in a bathtub, its branches springing through the fallen-in open roof.
>
> "Yes," he agreed. "You have found your poor place for the poor. For the little ones and your community of Sisters."
>
> We took his words as an affirmative omen.

She paused, then added: "The owner asked for nothing but a payment for a transfer agreement."[10]

Anne and the Jewish couple spoke together of their Jewish heritage and talked about their encounter with Father Oshida. Anne, a convert, said she felt a spiritual veil had been drawn across the eyes of Jews, so they could not see Christ. The couple nodded, seemingly understanding what she meant.

[10] Thus began Gray House, in the poor North End of Springfield, Massachusetts, which, beginning in 1982, has become a haven for poor families, providing food, clothing, and adult and after-school educational services. With more than one hundred volunteers, over five thousand people are helped by these programs each year.

Before they were married, they had discovered Father Oshida when he came to Jerusalem and gave a talk on *dabar* (Word-Event). This led them to practice *zazen* and go stay for a time at Takamori.

"He's so Jewish!" the Jewish mother exclaimed, with a happy toss of her glinting, light blond hair.

"Yes," said her dark-bearded husband, laughing out loud. "A real *mensch*. So sincere. Such integrity. A person who has the fiber of a bodhisattva, the depth of compassion in his very being, living for others, beyond self."

"Did you know what he did in Israel?" the husband asked. No one did.

He told us he learned Father Oshida would sometimes go to war-torn areas of the world to try to intervene, to serve as a peacemaker.

"One morning while visiting us, he went out our door, unbeknownst to us, and walked between Israeli-Palestinian lines when there was fighting going on, praying for a cease-fire."

"Yes," I said, "there is so much about Father Oshida that we shall never know. He always surprises you. For me every time Father Oshida celebrated the Eucharist with us and gave a homily or talk, I felt as though I was discovering Jesus for the first time, just like in 1976, when I first visited Takamori and experienced his Fire-Mass."

At the end of mealtime, Father Oshida gathered us once more in the *zendo* and encapsulated our pilgrimage.

"How wonderful it has been this week to recognize one another in communion, tears, and laughter," he smiled. "And at dinner last night, during the first mealtime with conversation, I listened to expressions of pure love and gratitude, forgiveness and joy, and felt the depth of the mystical body. Truly, a confirmation of hope and the degree of realization among us."

"Yes," one sister exclaimed softly. "We grasped what was shared throughout this week, what you stressed, Father. 'There is neither Jew nor Gentile, neither slave nor free, nor is there male and female, for you are all one in Christ Jesus' (Gal 3:28). That will stay with me always."

Father Oshida invited us to form a large circle and to join with him in holding hands with the persons on either side of us. After the weeklong *sesshin*, the silence was palpable, rich in *kavod*, the finger-light weight of being. Then he spoke:

"I must disappear. You must appear. Then he must appear. This is our spiritual joy. This is why we sit. We are motivated by joy. Joy is union with the Hand of God!"

"*Itadakimasu*," we all chanted, sharing bows with each person in the *zendo*, our palms folded in the *gasshō* of thanksgiving and blessing.

The room fell silent. We sat in a deep stillness. No one said another word.

After a long interval, Father Oshida broke the silence, softly humming in his evocative tenor voice a faintly familiar melody that I could not place.

Everyone was all ears, listening closely.

"When you sit alone," he said, "your song will come to you. Hum a sound, breathe a note, follow a line. Sing as you meditate."

He returned to humming his air, then began to sing in French, in question-and-answer stanzas, over and over. Almost immediately the bilingual Canadians joined in. Before long all of us caught on, singing the simple lines first in French, then in English when Oshida switched languages for us monolingual Americans.

Everyone was weeping as we sang.

Qui peut faire de la voile
sans vent ?
Qui peut ramer
sans rames ?
Et qui peut quitter
son ami
sans verser des larmes ?

Je peux faire de la voile
sans vent.
Je peux ramer
sans rames.
Et je peux quitter
mon ami
sans verser de larmes.

Who can sail
without wind?
Who can row
without oars?
And who can say goodbye
to a friend
without having tears?

I can sail
without wind.
I can row
without oars.
And I can say goodbye to a friend
without having tears

Years after the Oshida retreats in America, I learned that the song we sang with him in French and English at the end of a *sesshin* was of Scandinavian origin, known throughout the world as "But I cannot say goodbye to my friend without tears."

Father Oshida's changed the last line to "And I *can* say goodbye to a friend without having tears." The irony of this alteration of the lyrics was that in fact he knew it was impossible for him and for us not to shed tears. "Having tears" was his unidiomatic translation of the French *"verser des larmes"* [shed tears], which I suspect he did intentionally.

The changes were his touch.

The moment ceased. We got up to escort Father Oshida to his ride waiting outside and gathered around the car. He was carrying his impossibly small black leather satchel, with which he traveled around the world. Before he got in the vehicle, he wrote out the song for me in French and English on a scrap of paper. I have saved it these many years.

Suddenly, with a rapturous smile and a wave of his hand, he was gone.

September Meeting,
Last Days, Gleanings

The last time I was with Father Oshida was in 1981. One early summer day at my home in Massachusetts, I received a mysterious invitation from him to attend a weeklong meeting to be held from September 23 to 30, 1981, at Takamori Soan. The invitation was completely unexpected. His letter referred to a "September Meeting." Behind this innocuous title, Father Oshida was gathering peacemakers from around the world because he felt that the threat of a nuclear holocaust was extremely high. As a soldier in the Japanese army stationed in Japan during World War II, he must have been intimately aware of the horrific aftermath of America's dropping of two atomic bombs on Japan at Hiroshima and Nagasaki. In his subsequent life he became a prophet who was constantly issuing a wakeup call against nuclear disaster.

He was now inviting people from different countries who were engaged with the sufferings of humanity and the afflicted, who lived among the poor, served them, and were poor themselves. He felt their spirituality of service enabled them to hear the *Bat Kol*, the Voice of God. I was neither poor nor did I live among the poor. I suspect I was invited because Father Oshida knew of my work promoting a healing dialogue among women and men who experience the holocaust of abortion.

At the conference, Father Oshida welcomed us by inviting us to go on a spiritual journey together. "Both the afflicted and those who sit side by side with them as recipients of the gift of redemptive suffering for others are bearers of the cross on their way to the Father. Let us go on a pilgrimage together." His words were serious while his earnest face was smiling.

Then he clarified why we were gathering at the Takamori hermitage to meditate together. He felt we were experiencing a *kairos*, a time of crisis for the world.

> The desert of materialistic civilization is expanding exponentially, and I am deeply alarmed by the rampant development of nuclear weapons around the world and the lack of moral stamina to control them. Nature is being destroyed, and there is spiritual ruin accompanying this blight. Heads of state and leaders from various walks of life are groping in the dark with no clear sense of direction. I fear universal devastation throughout the earth. In the course that civilization is now taking, we feel something looming in which we anticipate the barren abyss where no one will be able to be saved from unfathomable darkness.

To an outsider who was unfamiliar with Father Oshida, his vision of the conference might have seemed quixotic, impractical, and overstated. But he went on to say that he was not interested in a phenomenal analysis of present reality. He wanted us to hear a call to listen to "the Voice concealed in history."

"Jesus asked for this assembly," he explained. "This is Bethlehem." He recalled the scripture, "Foxes have dens and birds have nests, but the Son of Man has no place to lay his head" (Luke 9: 58).

> We have been asked to come to a place where there is no pillow. It is the way to the Father, the cross. I was longing for a new horizon and perceived the time ripe for capable persons who shared others' pain and suffering and were living a spiritual life to undertake a different historical orientation. I invite you to leave yourselves behind on this pilgrimage, to disappear and obey the Voice of God. It is a duty of conscience.

I had been mystified that Father Oshida had invited me to the conference. When it came my turn to address the audience of spiritual pilgrims, I spoke about the "*Kodomo* in the Womb," the unborn child who could be aborted. Looking on Father Oshida's face as I spoke, I could see he was painfully reminded of the holocaust of the unborn in Japan. Their plight at home and around the world wounded him. The child in the womb was close to the heart of the September Conference.

Last Days

Father Oshida died eight years after he participated in the International Interfaith Pilgrimage for Peace and Life (1994–1995), an extraordinary walk from Auschwitz to Hiroshima to mark the fiftieth anniversary of the end of World War II. A journey of ten thousand miles through some eighteen countries scarred by old conflicts and the wounds of present-day wars, the pilgrimage was an act of collective remembering, reparation, compassion, and healing meant for the transformation of self and world.

As we know, Father Oshida struggled all his life with tuberculosis, which he called his "Zen master." He must have known that such a long peace journey would be too much for him. Following the pilgrimage, his health steadily declined until his death. Father Shigeto Vincent-Marie Oshida, OP, "returned to heaven" on November 6, 2003, while residing at Takamori. He was eighty-one years old.

When Father Oshida died, Sister Maria Kawasumi, a devoted member of the Takamori Soan community, sent this letter, dated December 22, 2003.

Peace in God.
As many of you may already know, Father Oshida went Home on the eve of November 6th, concluding his eight years struggling against cardiac failure. Having been in and out of hospital and unable to come back to live at Takamori Soan with its rigorous climate, he finally spent his last three

months at Takamori, enjoying the natural beauty of autumn in the mountains. Although there were times when he had to bear pain beyond description, he departed peacefully, passing over to the other shore in his last deep sleep. Everything being washed away, his expression was so beautiful that it impressed everyone who came to his side.

"All abandoning to God . . . God is wonderful . . ." he started murmuring two days before his death, looking at the falling leaves from his room. Then his murmur turned into a chant. "God is wonderful. God is wonderful. God is wonderful. Amen. Amen. Amen. Amen!"

They were the last words he uttered from the depth of his being.

Gleanings

By uniting in himself Buddhist insight and practice, Dominican spirituality, and the Catholic priesthood, Father Shigeto Oshida became one of the outstanding pioneers of interreligious dialogue, providing a concrete model of how the church and the faith of the individual believer can be transformed by encounters with other religions and spiritualities. The fruits of such encounters are the cross-fertilization and symbiosis of both and the awakening of the spiritual depths of each that are beyond all telling. As Walter Gardini writes, Buddhism's Ultimate Reality—Void, Nothing—is not a denial of God, but "is actually an assertion of the inaccessible and ineffable mystery of the Ultimate Reality."[1] In Shigeto Oshida, Zen practice radiates Christian radicalism.

Father Oshida's faith was transformed by living a union of spiritual traditions, initiating a way of faith and a pattern of prayer that was a blend of Buddhist and Christian mystical paths. He offered Catholics and other Christians a way to pene-

---

[1] Walter Gardini, "Prologue," in Claudia Mattiello, *Takamori Sōan: Teachings of Shigeto Oshida, a Zen Master* (Buenos Aires: Talleres Gráficos Color Efe, 2007).

trate the gospels by experiencing the Scriptures as Word-Event, serving the poor, celebrating the Eucharist, and praying/meditating with the body.

During his agony in the garden as Jesus awaited his arrest and execution, he asked Peter "So, could you not stay awake with me one hour?" (Matt 26:40). During a *sesshin*, Father Oshida called our experience of that Gethsemane a moment of true Zen. I interpret that to mean our experience of complete union with the Suffering Savior: Christ, Son of Mary, Son of Man, Son of God.

What might be another mystical encounter?

As mentioned earlier, once when I took him for a visit to the Nipponzan-Myōhōji Peace Pagoda in Leverett, Massachusetts, he fell into an ecstasy. As he slowly circled the Buddhist pagoda, stopping at four compass points to chant what I took to be Buddhist petitions or praises, he was a complete union of his past and his present, Zen monk and Catholic priest. Had I asked him if that was the case, he might well have responded, "It is not the sphere where you compare religions."

I have to remember that "Jesus in the Hands of Buddha" is my metaphor for Shigeto Oshida, not his. Mine is a "twosome" if you will, a dyad. His metaphor is union: Swimming in the waters flowing from the Unborn Sphere, experienced and expressed in his own inimitable way as Zen master and Catholic priest in love with Christ Jesus.

What comes to mind in trying to verbalize Father Oshida is his essence, a radical simplicity, a prophetic proclamation of *kairos* now. In his experience of conversion he became as though one on fire, which he made explicit in his "Fire-Mass" lit by the Holy Spirit. He met people where they were, whether in India, China, Japan, Europe, North America, or the Middle East, sensitive to their faiths or none, at home with their cultures. His favorite thing to do when visiting us was to hang out in some wayside country cafe and simply gaze in fascination at whomever or whatever was around him. And talk, of course. When some curious customer came up to him, eyeing this strange man wrapped in a black robe, Oshida and patron were suddenly best friends, smiling and laughing and sharing stories. "Toby's Hot Spot" he once crooned to a waitress in celebration of what to him was the wondrous name of her restaurant.

He was courageous, suffering his whole life with his Zen master, tuberculosis. He once bravely walked between warring lines of Arabs and Jews in the Holy Land seeking a laying down of arms.

Ironically, as we have seen, in his conversion to Christ and the Dominican priesthood he left behind the European Catholic Church, which he, like many Japanese, felt was a Western cultural import. For him, the church's institutional emphasis on law and bureaucracy distorted the gospel. There came a deep call to be alone, a wandering monk and itinerant priest, and, with the permission of his Dominican religious superior, to set out with total trust in God. After yet another stay in a TB sanatorium, he settled in at Takamori in the Japanese Alps as a hermit. As a community of spiritual pilgrims gathered around him, he became a star of inculturation espoused by Vatican II. His favorite church architecture was traditional Japanese, a three-foot-thick thatched chapel roof made of rice stalks, a wooden plank set on the floor for an altar, a fire lit in a *hibachi* at the moment of the consecration of the Eucharist.

Father William Johnston's Ash Wednesday Charismatic Zen retreat brought me to the discovery of Shigeto Oshida and Takamori in 1976. Almost immediately upon my arrival there, in the words of St. Paul, "the scales fell from my eyes" (Acts 9:18), and I could see, spiritually speaking. At Father Oshida's hermitage I encountered a lifestyle of total simplicity and a living embodiment of Jesus' teachings and gospel values. The only rule at Takamori was The Rule of No Rule: The sole exception was that liars were not welcome. Everyone else was. That meant Jews, Muslims, Buddhists, and Christians, the healthy and the sick, believers and nonbelievers, but especially the poor. Differences and warts were worn down by daily physical labor, *zazen*, and Father Oshida's Fire-Mass.

My religious faith came alive through the discovery of an experiential spirituality, the discipline of breathing, chanting, listening, and yielding to the Spirit within my body and soul. From time to time, Jesus comes alive for me in receiving the Eucharist or experiencing a scriptural Word-Event but most especially when visiting the sick. I do not pretend to be a mystic but I hear Shigeto Oshida's words ring in my ears:

"Let God take you to the abyss."

"Jesus is a man made for seduction by the sufferings of others."

"Look at the flower. It is Jesus."

"In *zazen* we sit on the cross."

"Each of us is a star born on the cross from far away."

"Die where 'I' disappears for those who do not believe us."

"Die when you come to Holy Communion."

He embodied emptiness (*kung*) and letting go (*wu wei*). He lived charity and interior obedience. Being with him was like going on retreat with Jesus and Buddha.

In Father Oshida I experienced the revelation of Christ through Zen. In his *Omidō* Fire-Mass his face shone with the illumination of Jesus. Though he sometimes had to catch his balance standing in two different boats, Catholic and Buddhist, form and practice were one with his faith in Christ, whether he was at home or abroad, in Takamori or Jerusalem. His life as Catholic priest and Zen master was ignited by a single flame. To borrow the words of Ama Samy, an Indian Jesuit roshi, he was "a rare bird." He believes that "such persons are the salt of interreligious dialogue," and he and theologian Paul Knitter might think of them as paragons of transformation rather than translation.[2] Father Oshida did not use Zen simply to deepen

---

[2] Ama Samy (Aru Maria Arokiasamy), SJ, studied with Yamada Kōun Roshi, who authorized him to teach Zen. His Zen school and retreat center, Bodhi Sangha, is in Perumalmalai, India. See Ama Samy, "Interreligious Dialogue: Beyond Translation, Beyond Religion," *Dilatato Corde* 1, no. 2 (2011). See also Pat van Boeckel, "Zen and the Art of Compassion," Vimeo video, https://www.lovelandzen.org/filmzencompassion (accessed November 5, 2022).

or broaden Christianity and Christian spirituality. As a Zen master, he called others to experience transfiguration and conversion in their encounter with Jesus, the Savior of the world.

As I have learned from the prodigious Catholic scholar and specialist in Buddhology, Robert Magliola, hidden within or palpably felt in transfiguration through Buddhist-Christian encounter, there is "samenesses and irreducible difference"— for example, rebirth as opposed to one life span only, self-power in contrast to other-power (God), and no self versus eternal self. As one who has trained for long periods under Asian Buddhist monastics, Magliola has discovered that while the founding doctrines of Buddhism and Christianity are contradictory, the effects generated by these contradictory doctrines are often similar. For example, Buddhist "compassion" (*karuṇā*) and Christian "compassion" express themselves in very similar behaviors ("samenesses") but are generated by contrary founding doctrines.[3]

As for myself, I call on Buddha to invigorate my meditation in morning prayer. I think of him with utter awe and the deepest reverence and respect. I often interiorize the koan Joshu Sasaki Roshi gave the monks during a *sesshin* at St. Joseph's Abbey: "How do you experience God when you look upon Christ hanging on the Cross?"

"How do you experience your True Self seeing Jesus crucified?" he repeated, over and over again during *dokusan*, the moment when each monk answered this koan when sitting alone before the roshi. "How do you experience God and your True Self when you see the butterfly?" he queried as he caught

---

[3] Robert Magliola email to Lucien Miller, July 9, 2022. See Magliola's seminal study, *Facing Up to Real Doctrinal Difference: How Some Thought-Motifs from Derrida Can Nourish the Catholic-Buddhist Encounter* (Kettering, OH: Angelico Press, 2014). Through the application of the deconstruction literary theory of Jacques Derrida, Magliola shows that these differences can nourish one another.

me sitting painfully on my zafu pillow distractedly gazing out a window at a yellow swallowtail butterfly flitted by.

To pun on Paul Knitter's *Without Buddha I Could Not Be a Christian*,[4] with Buddha I can be a better Christian or at least try to be; one who might experience Jesus in the Eucharist, or, in the mind's eye and the heart's contemplation, watch him making a breakfast fire on the beach of the Sea of Galilee after the resurrection. The point is experience, the *sine qua non* for a mystic, the precious though unpredictable complement or companion for the person of faith.

Interiorizing Buddhist thought and Buddhist contemplation, I practice "just sitting" or "silent illumination" (*shikantaza*)—contemplative prayer, if you will; the way of mystics—through which from time to rare time I experience Jesus in the Eucharist, at home and abroad, in family, nature, and life. In the end I have to say, I have been sitting for fifty years and am still very much a beginner. *Deo gratias*.

May you be transformed by your encounter with Shigeto Oshida, OP, as I dare to say I have, or at least hope I have. May your faith or lack of faith be transfigured so that you can "taste and see" (Ps 34:8) self and other in a new light.

Be not afraid.

Blessings and Memories

On October 12, 2015, a little community of contemplatives and peacemakers—Buddhist monks, a Catholic and an Episcopal priest, and Catholic sisters and laity—gathered in our back yard for a "Blessings Day" to honor the memory of Father Oshida by vowing never to forget the *anawim*, born and unborn, who have gone before us. It was a mystical moment of union on a glorious New England fall day, a profound religious

---

[4] Paul Knitter, *Without Buddha I Could Not Be a Christian* (Oxford: Oneworld, 2009).

experience for a tiny United Nations convocation of pilgrims and friends, an interfaith Pentecost.

For me, it was a dream come true.

The centerpiece of the Takamori West Memorial is an upright black locust log from the farm of our neighbor, Jim Doubleday. Japanese artist Tom Matsuda shaped the log, affixed it to a long flagstone from an ancient New England stone wall, and inscribed on it a poem that is an exact replica of the original I discovered on my first visit to the Remembrance Wood at Takamori. It reads:

限りなき　なみだの海に　消えず　立たなむ 茂人
"Kagiri naki namida no umi ni kiezu tatanamu" Shigeto

We shall stand,
without disappearing
in the infinite sea
of tears[5]

In the adjoining woods, some thirty or forty feet away from the centerpiece is a trail sign created by graphic artist and book designer, Anne Martens. It bears a scarred image of the "Bombed Mary" (*"Hibakusha* Mary" or *"Urakami* Mary") that miraculously survived the second American nuclear holocaust of World War II at Nagasaki, Japan, on August 9, 1945.

The dedication on the sign reads:

> *For the Holy Innocents, Born and Unborn,*
> *Destroyed in America's Wars.*

An accompanying text explains the provenance of this image.

---

[5] The English translation is by Father Oshida.

Photo designer: Anne Martens

*"Urakami Mary" is the blackened head of the
full-length painted wooden Madonna
discovered in the ruins of the Urakami Cathedral
of the Immaculate Conception
razed by the Nagasaki Atomic Bomb,
cindering worshippers and priests inside.
Her eyeless face is exquisite—the beauty of the Virgin Survivor—
a face of ultimate sorrow, understanding, compassion
and forgiveness.*

At the base of the sign are biblical and liturgical excerpts honoring the Holy Innocents:

"The earth will reveal the blood upon her,
and no longer conceal her slain."
Isaiah 26:21

"Awake and sing, you who sleep in the earth,
for the dew of the LORD is a dew of light."
Isaiah 26:19

"They skip with joy like lambs, for you have set them free.
Earth resounds with the echo of their song."
Divine Office, Feast of the Holy Innocents, December 28

Our ecumenical interfaith East-West blessing was led by Abbot Gyoway Kato and two of his Buddhist monks from the New England Peace Pagoda in Leverett, Massachusetts. They belong to the Nippozan-Myōhōji Buddhist Order, dedicated to promoting peace and nonviolence throughout the world. The Buddhist monks beat hand drums while chanting the Daimoku, *"Namu Myōhō Renge Kyō."* "Glory to the Sutra of the Lotus of the Supreme Law." Following this chant, the Christian participants recited the Our Father, the Hail Mary, and verses from the Psalms.

The trail sign points to the third feature of the memorial, the quarter-mile-long "Holy Innocents Trail," which winds through the Remembrance Wood behind our home in a figure eight, a symbol of eternity. It is dedicated to the *anawim* in Asia and America destroyed by us humans through war, genocide, abortion, and terror.

At the entrance to the trail, we shared dedicatory prayers of petition.

Then we began our walk, pausing along the way to bless, chant, and pray together before Japanese artist Tom Matsuda's carved "Jesus in the Hands of Buddha," which I had set out on the forest floor.

Along our meditative march, we heard the distant shouts and cries of joy of the Pelham Elementary School children playing during their afternoon recess on the other side of Remembrance Wood. As we stepped forth, their ecstatic voices were a poignant accompaniment to the haunting recitative chant of the monks, blessing every leaf, tree, and stone.

May our prayers, chants, and meditations, as well as those of future visitors to this memorial, be acts of *tikkun olam*, the Jewish concept of "repairing," "making good," and "rescuing" of our world.[6]

In memory of Father Shigeto Oshida and to honor him,

> May we be pilgrim spirits together
> in word and deed
> swimming in our underground streams
> flowing from the Unborn Sphere

---

[6] George Steiner, "To Speak of Walter Benjamin," in *Benjamin Studies: Perception and Experience in Modernity* (Amsterdam: Rodopi, 2002), 22. Citation from Christopher Pramuk, *At Play in Creation* (Collegeville MN: Liturgical Press, 2015), 79.

The Greatest Accomplishment

What is the greatest accomplishment?
It's to grow old with a peaceful heart,
To rest when we desire to work,
To keep quiet when we want to blubber,
To hope when we know disappointment,
To carry one's cross in quietness and obedience.
Do not feel jealousy when the young stride on a
    highway of God,
Find contentment not in working to help others
but in receiving help from them.
Stay kind and graceful when, in weakness,
You're no longer useful.
The heavy burden of old age is a gift from God.
With it we prepare our tired soul for the very last
    time,
To travel to our true home.
It takes enormous effort to loosen piece by piece
the chain that connects us to the world.
When we cannot do it anymore, accept it with
    humility.
God leaves us the best work at the end.
It's prayer.
Our hands may shrivel but they can be held
    together to pray
Over those whom we love,
Seeking for God's mercy to the very last moment.

And at the end, we will hear the voice of God,
"Come Friend. Be with me."

Hermann Heuvers, SJ[1]
Translated by Chisato Kitagawa

---

[1] Father Heuvers was Father Oshida's spiritual director and guided him to the priesthood.

ACKNOWLEDGMENTS

Chisato Kitagawa, my dear friend and mentor, professor of Japanese and Episcopal priest, without whom this book could not have been written, and his beloved wife Mary, whose warmth, friendship, and spiritual insight have ever touched my heart;

Fran Howe, whose constant encouragement helped me keep writing, and whose astute critical sense taught me to read and see;

Susan Solinsky, poet and precious friend, whose writerly wisdom and graciousness mentored me along my long stumbling path;

Sisters of St. Joseph Jane Morrissey and Cathy Homrok, whose lifelong friendships have graced my life, and whose selfless help enlivened an Oshida *sesshin* at Mary House, Spencer, Massachusetts;

Forever friend Marty Slavkovski, whose sharp eye and repeated readings of the entire manuscript saved it from myriad typos, spelling snags, and pitfalls;

Timothy Radcliffe, OP, Master of the Order of Preachers, 1992–2001, whose Foreword has graced this book with a deep grasp of dwelling and abiding in Shigeto Oshida's "word-event," and a fond personal encounter with his joyous being;

Dominican Fathers Louis Roy, OP, who blessed my initial steps along the Buddhist-Catholic way, and John Allard, OP, spiritual guide;

My ever-patient, insightful editor Father William Skudlarek, OSB, who guided, inspired, and encouraged my writing every step of the way;

Hans Christoffersen, editorial director of Liturgical Press, for his astute stewardship designing this book;

Former students Russell Keziere and now Catholic Worker Janet Ward, who both grasped the depths of contemplative literature, East and West;

Jonathan Montaldo, Merton master, writer, editor, spiritual guide, sage, and empathetic editor of *The Hidden Side of the Mountain*, my initial writing on Shigeto Oshida;

Dan Robb, friend and neighbor, whose experience as writer and manuscript reader guided me through early stages of this book;

Distinguished friends of the ROMEOS (Retired Old Men Eating Out Society), Richard Sinkoski, calm, fair-minded discussant and erudite guide on all things Catholic; Bill Moebius, UMass colleague, poet, and inspired pianist; provident commentator and Renaissance man Simon James; good as gold pal Roy Baltharzard; Michael Konstan, my personal Buddhism guide, who introduced me to Roshi Cynthia Taberner and the Day Star Zendo in Wrentham, Massachusetts, founded by her and Trappist monk Kevin Jiun Hunt, residing priest for the Trappistine Sisters of Mount St. Mary's Abbey in Wrentham;

And last but really first, my wife Bonnie, the heart and clear head of our youthful marriage made in heaven, whose love, intuition, and wisdom have blessed my life for sixty-plus years.

VITA

Chronology Sources

English Chronology, 1922–1981:

> Shigeto Oshida and Joseph Domjan, *The White Deer* (Ryogoku, Tokyo: WAGO, 1986).

> Hiroshige Watanabe, OP, email to Lucien Miller, April 4, 2014.

> Family background information from Professor Chisato Kitagawa interview with Sister Maria Kawasumi and Father Hiroshige Watanabe, OP, June 5, 2015, Takamori Soan. Email to Lucien Miller, June 5, 2015.

Japanese Chronology, 1922–2003:

> Hiroshsige Watanabe, OP, email to Chisato Kitagawa, August 28, 2014. English translation and notes: Professor Chisato Kitagawa.

1922 (Taishō 11). Born January 15 in Namamugi, Yokohama, the youngest of six children. His father was businessman and Soto Zen Buddhist who was baptized before he died. His mother belonged to a distinguished Shinto family. Her father was Chief Shinto Priest at Fuji Sengen Jinja 富士浅間神社, one of the shrines connected to Mount Fuji. She was baptized not too long after Father Oshida became a member of the Dominican Order. Soon after his birth, Oshida's family moves to the Shibuya Ward in Tokyo.

1942 (Showa 17). Graduates from *Dai-ichi Kotō Gakkō*, "First National College," a prestigious two-year college for a select number of exceptional male students following six years of high school and prior to their enrollment at a university or four-year college.

1943 (Showa 18). Encounters Father Hermann Heuvers, SJ, a Jesuit priest and his future spiritual director. Awakening to the faith, he is baptized in October and in December is drafted into the army and assigned to the Antiaircraft Corps of the Edogawa Army Division.

1944 (Showa 19). Enters Officers' Training School and receives training in antisubmarine radar. He is then transferred to the Akatsuki Division, Army Transportation Corps, and graduates that same year.

1945 (Showa 20). Discharged from the army at the end of World War II.

1946 (Showa 21). Enrolls in the Philosophy Department of Tokyo University.

1948 (Showa 23). Nearly drowns while swimming in the ocean at Arahama beach, Miyagi Prefecture. Saved by an American GI who gives him artificial respiration, he is hospitalized at Tohoku University Hospital in Sendai with an acute attack of tuberculosis and gangrene of lungs. Discharged from the hospital, he is transferred to the National Miyagi Prefectural Sanatorium in Sendai. He suffers recurrences of lung diseases for the rest of his life.

1950 (Showa 25). Discharged from National Miyagi Hospital, he immediately takes up residence in Canadian Dominican Monastery at Sendai.

1951 (Showa 26). Graduates from Tokyo University and enters the Order of Preachers (OP) to begin his formation as a Dominican friar.

1952 (Showa 27). Suffers a relapse of lung disease and reenters the National Miyagi Sanatorium.

1953 (Showa 28). Is discharged from the sanatorium in April.

1955 (Showa 30). Inspired by spiritual life of novice master, Father Bernard Tarte, OP, he makes his first profession of vows as a Dominican friar at the Sendai Monastery.

1958 (Showa 33). Enters the Dominican Theological Seminary, Ottawa, Canada.

1961 (Showa 36). Is ordained to the priesthood on April 8. His tuberculosis worsens soon after ordination and he is hospitalized at Hôpital Maisonneuve Montreal where he meets a mystic lumberjack. Moved to a convalescent center in a virgin forest on the shore of Lac Edward, he receives correspondence and simple gifts from an unidentified European female mystic.

1962 (Showa 37). Returns to Japan and is admitted to St. Mary's International Hospital and then transferred to Sakuramachi Hospital in Musashi Koganei.

1963 (Showa 38). Part of his right lung is removed at Sakuramachi Hospital. He recuperates at Koike Hospital, Fujimi township, Nagano Prefecture.

1964 (Showa 39). Is discharged from the hospital.

1963–1964 Serves as a curate at Sukegawa Catholic Church, Fukushima Prefecture. After six months there, he receives permission from his religious superior, Father Bernard M. Trahan, OP, Japanese regional prior of the Canadian Province of the Dominicans and pastor at Sukegawa Catholic Church, to leave Dominican conventual life while remaining a Dominican priest.

1964 (Showa 39). Lives at two different places in Sakai-mura, a village adjacent to Fujimi-cho. While at the village or following his stay there, he lives in an uninhabited Kannon temple at Takamori and discovers its spring, "Koizumi." He is again hospitalized in Tokyo in October. In December he receives a phone call from the village he had lived in informing him that the land on which Koizumi was located is for sale. Having received permission from the hospital to look at the land, he decides to buy it, trusting that God will provide the money to make the purchase. The money arrives, and life at the "Takamori Soan" hermitage begins.

1965 (Showa 40). Publishes his first book, *Bara no Madoi,*
   A Gathering of Roses (Kyoto: Veritas). He leaves Takamori
   to serve as curate of Sukegawa Catholic Church,
   Fukushima Prefecture, and returns to Takamori
   six months later.

1967 (Showa 42). Attends the first Zen and Christianity
   Dialogue Conference held in Oiso, Kanagawa Prefecture.
   Dom Jean Leclercq, OSB, French monastic historian and
   theologian, visits Takamori Soan.

1968 (Showa 43). December, attends East-West Monastic
   Dialogue Conference of Benedictines and Cistercians in
   Bangkok, Thailand. Meets Thomas Merton, OCSO, before
   Merton's sudden death at the conference. In February,
   visits India on his way back to Japan.

1969 (Showa 44). Publishes a series of autobiographical writings,
   Michi Sugara, Along the Way (Kyoto: Veritas).

1970 (Showa 45). Murray Rogers, Anglican priest and charismatic pioneer in East-West religious encounter, visits
   Takamori Soan and invites Oshida to visit the celebrated
   Jyotiniketan "House of Light" community, a Christian
   counterpart to Mahatma Gandhi's ashram that Rogers
   and his family established in India, 1954.

1971 (Showa 46). Travels through India and meets the French
   Benedictine monk Abhishiktananda (Henri Le Saux), Sara
   Grant, and other Christian spiritual leaders and Hindu
   saints. Abhishiktananda, a pioneer of Hindu-Christian
   dialogue, adopted a sannyasa life of renunciation and
   abandonment in accordance with Hindu Indian tradition.
   Sara Grant, a religious of the Sacred Heart of Jesus (RSCJ),
   was a British Indologist, Christian missionary, and
   innovator in interreligious dialogue and inculturation in
   India.

1972 (Showa 47). Attends the Canadian Regional Conference
   of the Dominican Order. Travels throughout Europe and
   the United States to determine if it would be beneficial to

send young Japanese seminarians abroad for research and spiritual training.

1973 (Showa 48). Invited to Israel to promote friendship between Arab and Jewish people, he visits the Philippines, India, Vietnam, Hong Kong, and South Korea en route.

1974 (Showa 49). Participates in dialogues with Palestinians in Lebanon and with Arabs and Jews in Israel. He observes civil culture and people's lives in Vietnam and has conversations with religious leaders in Hong Kong. In South Korea he meets Ham Sok-hon (咸錫憲, 함 석 헌), the "Gandhi of Korea," National Cultural Figure and leader in the Society of Friends (Quaker). He also meets Ji Hak-soon (池 学 淳, 지 학순), Roman Catholic bishop, leader of a democratic resistance movement against president and dictator Park Chung-hee (1917–1979), and initiator of a campaign for human rights, especially for factory workers. In the United States, he meets Hungarian artist József Domján for the first time.

1975 (Showa 50). Travels throughout Europe, particularly Poland, visiting churches. On the way home, he visits Vietnam, the Philippines, Saipan, and Hong Kong and meets with indigenous people in Saipan and Mangyan tribes in the Philippines.

1976 (Showa 51). Publishes *Harami to Oto, Conception and Sound* (Kyoto: Veritas) and visits the Igorot tribe in the Philippines.

1977 (Showa 52). Publishes *Ai no Mizu, Indigo Water* (Kyoto: Veritas) and travels to Hong Kong, Canada, the United States, and the Philippines, conducting retreats. He again meets Domjan and leads the first retreat (*sesshin*) at Mary House, near St. Joseph's Abbey, Spencer, Massachusetts, August 21–27.

1978 (Showa 53). Travels to the Philippines, Bangladesh, and Taiwan.

1979 (Showa 54). Gives retreats in the Philippines and again lives with the Igorot people.

1980 (Showa 55). Travels to Hong Kong, the United States, the Philippines, and Taiwan. While attending the International Catholic Mission Congress in Manila, he meets African leaders. He conducts a second retreat (*sesshin*) at Mary House, August 18–24.

1981 (Showa 56). Convenes the "September Conference," September 23–30 (emergency meeting of world spiritual leaders at Takamori Soan) and publishes *"Kugatsu Kaigi"—Sekai Seishin Shidoosha, Kinkyuu no Tsudoi, "The September Conference"—The Emergency Meeting of the Spiritual Leaders of the World* (Kyoto: Veritas, 1981).

1983 (Showa 58). Publishes *Tooi Manazashi, A Far Away Look* (Tokyo: Chiyūsha, 1983). Conducts a third retreat (*sesshin*) at Holy Cross Abbey, Berryville, Virginia, in mid-August.

1985 (Showa 60). Publishes *Inori no Sugata-ni Mu no Kaze-ga Fuku* 「祈りの姿に無の風が吹く」, *A Figure Praying Amidst the Wind of Nothing,"Nothingness" or "Emptiness."* (Tokyo: Chiyūsha, 1985).

1986 (Showa 61). Publishes poems in *Shiroi Shika, The White Deer.* (Tokyo: WAGO). Woodcuts: Joseph Domjan. Poems: Shigeto Oshida.

1990 (Heisei 2). Organizes Asian Bishops' Conference, which meets at Takamori.

1994–1995 (Heisei 6–7). Participates in portions of the "Interfaith Pilgrimage for Peace and Life," from Auschwitz, Poland to Nagasaki, Japan (December 8, 1994–August 9, 1995). Commemorating the fiftieth anniversary of the Hiroshima and Nagasaki atomic bombings and the end of World War II, pilgrims bore witness to suffering in contemporary war zones. Organized by Brother Gyoshu Sasamori from the Buddhist Nipponzan-Myōhōji peace order, the pilgrimage included American, European,

South American, and Japanese lay participants, and spanned roughly ten thousand miles, three thousand on foot, through troubled areas from Auschwitz to Vienna and Eastern Europe (Croatia, Bosnia, and Serbia), the Middle East (Israel, the Gaza Strip, the West Bank, Jordan, and Iraq), then India and Southeast Asia (Malaysia, Thailand, Cambodia, Vietnam, and the Philippines), and finally Hiroshima and Nagasaki.

Oshida was hospitalized after the march. Thereafter, he required constant medical care.

2000 (Heisei 12). Publishes *Ryooshi no Kokuhaku—Sei Yohane Fukuinsho, Confession of a Fisherman—St. John's Gospel,* "Private version" (*Shikaban*—a personal translation, handwritten, printed on silk screen).

2003 (Heisei 15). Publishes *Ryooshi no Kokuhaku—Sei Yohane Fukuinsho, Confession of a Fisherman—St. John's Gospel,* "Public version" (*Fukyuuban*). Returned to heaven, November 6, 2003.

BIBLIOGRAPHY

English Writing and Lectures

"Evangelization and Inculturation." Manuscript. 10 pages.

"Evangelization and Inculturation" and "Zen: The Mystery of the Word and Reality." *Japan Missionary Bulletin* 45 (1991): 153–59. Reprint: *Monastic Interreligious Dialogue Bulletin*, ed. Mark Delery, OCSO. Vol. 75 (October 2005).

"The Good News from Sinanosakai," 1965. Oshida wrote in Japanese. English translation made after his death. Unpublished manuscript.

"I Shall Meet You in Galilee." In *The Dominican Way*, edited by Lucette Verboven, 189–200. London and New York: Continuum, 2011.

"A Little Note for the Assembly: Word-Idea Word-Event." "September Meeting," Takamori International Conference, September 23–30, 1981. Takamori Soan, Japan.

"Message to the Assembly of Auschwitz." Fr. Shigeto Oshida. Interfaith Pilgrimage for Peace and Life. Newsletter. Vol. 1 (1995). http://www.jyunrei.net/jyunrei95e1.htm (accessed November 5, 2022).

"The Mystery of the Word and the Reality." In *Toward a New Age in Mission: The Good News of God's Kingdom; To The Peoples of Asia*, 208–16. International Congress on Mission (IMC). Manila, December 2–7, 1979. Vol. 2, book 3. Manila: Theological Conference Office, 1981.

"What Is Faith?" Unpublished manuscript. No date. 10 pages.

White Deer. Woodcuts by Joseph Domjan [József Domján]. Poems by Shigeto Oshida. Tokyo, Japan: The Board of Publications, The United Church of Christ in Japan, 2015.

"Zenna." Manuscript article for the International Mission Congress, Manila, Philippines. December 2–6, 1979.

Japanese Writing

Source Chisato Kitagawa

Ai no Mizu「藍の水」(*Indigo Water*). Kyoto: Shisōan Veritas, 1977.

Bara no Madoi「ばらのまどい」(*A Gathering of Roses*). Kyoto: Shisōan Veritas, 1965.

Harami to Oto「孕みと音」(*Conception and Sound*). Kyoto: Shisōan Veritas, 1976.

Hitori no Wakamono no Miteita Koto「一人の若者の観ていたコト」(*What One Young Man Saw—St. Mark's Gospel*). Translated by Shigeto Oshida, Sr. Maria Kawasumi, and Hiroshige Watanabe. Kyoto: Shisōan Veritas, 2008.

Inori no Sugata-ni Mu no Kaze-ga Fuku「祈りの姿に無の風が吹く」(*A Figure Praying Amidst the Wind of Nothing, "Nothingness" or "Emptiness"*). Tokyo: Chiyūsha, 1985.

Ishi no Kohogi no Sho 押田成人訳、ルカ福音「医師のことほぎの書」(*A Book of Praise by a Medical Doctor—St. Luke's Gospel*). Translated by Sr. Maria Kawasumi and Fr. Hiroshige Watanabe. Nagano: Shisōan, 2013.

"Kugatsu Kaigi"—Sekai Seishin Shidoosha, Kinkyuu no Tsudoi (*"The September Conference"—The Emergency Meeting of the Spiritual Leaders of the World*). Kyoto: Shisōan Veritas, 1981.

Michi Sugara「道すがら」(*Along the Way*). Kyoto: Shisōan Veritas, 1969.

Ryooshi no Kokuhaku—Sei Yohane Fukuinsho, 私家版『漁師の告白聖ヨハネ福音書』(*Confession of a Fisherman—St. John's Gospel*). Handwritten translation printed on silk screen. Private publication, 2000.

Ryooshi no Kokuhaku「漁師の告白」(*Confession of a Fisherman*). Kyoto: Shisōan Veritas, 2003.

Shiroi Shika「白い鹿」(*The White Deer*). Coauthored with József Domján. Kyoto: Shisōan Veritas, 1981.

Tooi Manazashi「遠いまなざし」(*A Far Away Look*). Tokyo: Chiyūsha, 1983.

Zeiri no Satori to Nagame「税吏の悟りとながめ」(*Satori—What A Tax Collector Saw—a Tax Collector's Awakening. St. Matthew's Gospel*). Translated by Sr. Maria Kawasumi and Hiroshige Watanabe. Kyoto: Shisōan Veritas, 2010.

Secondary Sources

Amaldas, Swami. "The Breath of God—To the Zen Center of Soan, Japan." Translated by Sarah Schwartzberg. *Monastic Interreligious Dialogue Bulletin* 10 (February 1981).

Åmell, Katrin. "The Dominican Vincent Oshida Shigeto—A Buddhist Who Has Encountered Christ." *La vie spirituelle* 731 (1999): 355–68.

Åmell, Katrin. *"Zenna": Shigeto Oshida, en japansk dominikan*. Stockholm: Sankta Ingrids stift., Dominikansystrarna, 1993.

Bade, William Frederic. *The Life and Letters of John Muir*. Boston: Houghton Mifflin, 1924.

Berrigan, Daniel. "Three Conferences for the Novices, Abbey of Gethsemani." *The Merton Seasonal* (Fall 2016).

Bradshaw, David. "The *Logoi* of Beings in Greek Patristic Thought." In *Toward an Ecology of Transfiguration: Orthodox Christian Perspectives on Environment, Nature, and Creation*, edited by John Chryssavgis and Bruce V. Foltz, 9–13. New York: Fordham University Press, 2013.

Brown, Dan, Lisa Roche, Skip Schiel, and Dan Turner, eds. "Interfaith Pilgrimage for Peace and Life 1995." Newsletter. Vol. 1, 2, "Voices from Auschwitz"; Vol. 3, 4, "Voices from Eastern Europe." http://www.jyunrei.net/jyunrei95e3.htm (accessed November 5, 2022).

Chupungco, Anscar. *Cultural Adaptation of the Liturgy*. Mahwah, NJ: Paulist Press, 1982.

Congar, Yves. *I Believe in the Holy Spirit*. 3 vols. New York: Seabury, 1983. French orig. 1979.

Egan, Harvey. "Reflections of Saint Faustina," *Budhi: A Journal of Ideas and Culture* 6, nos. 2 and 3 (2002): 189–221.

Enger, Leif. *Peace like a River*. New York: Atlantic Monthly Press, 2001.

Ernst, Cornelius. *The Theology of Grace*. Notre Dame, IN: Fides Publishers, 1974.

Graham, Douglas J. M. *Dürer and Domjan: Over Fifty Works by Two Masters of the Woodcut to Honor Domjan's Two Hundred and Fiftieth Exhibition*. New York: Graham Collection, 1972.

Grayston, Donald. *Thomas Merton and the Noonday Demon: The Camaldoli Correspondence*. Cambridge: Lutterworth Press, 2015.

Hackett, David G. *The Silent Dialogue: Zen Letters to a Trappist Abbot*. New York: Continuum, 1996.

Hampl, Patricia. *The Florist's Daughter*. Orlando: Harcourt, 2007.

Harada, Katsu et. al., eds. Reports from the "Interfaith Pilgrimage for Peace and Life 1995." *Newsletter Jyunrei* 3, 4, no. 4 (1995). Tokyo: Meiji Gakuin University. http://www.jyunrei.net/jyunrei95e3.htm (accessed November 5, 2022).

Hergott, Fabrice. *Rouault*. Translated by Richard Lewis Rees. Paris: A. Michel, 1991.

Keating, Thomas. *Reflections on the Unknowable*. New York: Lantern Books, 2014.

Kitagawa, Joseph Mitsuo. *The Christian Tradition: Beyond Its European Captivity*. Philadelphia: Trinity Press International, 1992.

Knitter, Paul. *Without Buddha I Could Not Be a Christian*. Oxford: Oneworld, 2009.

Kowalska, Maria Faustina. *Diary of Saint Maria Faustina Kowalska: Divine Mercy in My Soul*. Stockbridge, MA: Marian Press, 2014.

Magliola, Robert. *Facing Up to Real Doctrinal Difference: How Some Thought-Motifs from Derrida Can Nourish the Catholic-Buddhist Encounter*. Kettering, OH: Angelico Press, 2014.

Mattiello, Claudia. *Takamori Sōan. Ensenanzas de Shigeto Oshida un maestro Zen*. Buenos Aires: Ediciones Continente, 2005.

Mattiello, Claudia. *Takamori Sōan: Teachings of Shigeto Oshida, a Zen Master*. Buenos Aires: Talleres Gráficos Color Efe, 2007.

McGilchrist, Iain. *The Master and His Emissary: The Divided Brain and the Making of the Western World*. New exp. ed. New Haven and London: Yale University Press, 2019.

Merton, Thomas. "Answers for Hernan Lavin Cerda: On War, Technology, and the Intellectual." *The Merton Annual* 2 (1989): 5–12.

Merton, Thomas. *The Asian Journal of Thomas Merton*. Edited by Naomi Burton, Brother Patrick Hart, and James Laughlin. New York: New Directions, 1973.

Merton, Thomas. "In the Wilderness." *The Merton Seasonal* 40, no. 2 (Summer 2015).

Merton, Thomas. "Lecture Notes on Theology and Mysticism." *Merton and Hesychasm: The Prayer of the Heart; The Eastern Church*. Edited by Bernadette Dieker and Jonathan Montaldo. Louisville, KY: Fons Vitae, 2003.

Merton, Thomas. *Mystics and Zen Masters*. New York: Farrar, Strauss and Giroux, 1967.

Merton, Thomas. *A Search for Solitude: Pursuing the Monk's True Life*. San Francisco: HarperSanFrancisco, 1996.

Merton, Thomas. *The Seven Storey Mountain*. New York: Harcourt, Brace, 1948.

Merton, Thomas. *The Wisdom of the Desert: Sayings from the Desert Fathers of the Fourth Century*. New York: New Directions, 1970.

Miller, Lucien. *Alone for Others: The Life of Tony Walsh*. Toronto: Community Concern Associates Ltd., 1987.

Miller, Lucien. *The Hidden Side of the Mountain: Encounters with Wisdom's Poor and Holy*. Louisville, KY: Fons Vitae, 2021.

Miller, Lucien. "Poetry as Contemplation: T'ao Ch'ien's 'Homing' (Guei qulai ci, 歸 去 來 辭), and William Wordsworth's 'Tintern Abbey.'" *Journal of the Institute of Chinese Studies* 6, no. 2 (December, 1973): 563–84.

Miller, Lucien. "Wisdom's Flowering Cherry Tree: The Charismatic Zen of William Johnston, SJ." *Dilatato Corde* 11, no. 2 (2021). https://dimmid.org/index.asp?Type=B_BASIC &SEC=%7b79A59B4F-013C-4E0D-B86B-80D28C12A258%7d (accessed November 5, 2022). Also in *Buddhist-Christian Studies* 42 (2022) with the title: "Wisdom's Flowering Cherry: William Johnston's Charismatic Zen."

Mornand, Pierre. *Domjan: In the Forest of The Golden Dragon.* Tuxedo Park, NY: Opus, 1973.

Morson, John, and Hilary Costello. *Guerric d'Igny: Sermons.* 2 vols. *Sources Chrétiennes.* Paris: Cerf, 1970, 1973.

Mott, Michael. *The Seven Mountains of Thomas Merton.* Boston: Houghton Mifflin, 1984.

Parmenter, Charles. *History of Pelham, Massachusetts, from 1738 to 1898.* Press of Carpenter and Morehouse, 1898.

Pennington, Basil. "Thomas Merton and Byzantine Spirituality." *Merton and Hesychasm: The Prayer of the Heart; The Eastern Church.* Edited by Bernadette Dieker and Jonathan Montaldo. Louisville, KY: Fons Vitae, 2003.

Pope Francis. *Evangelii Gaudium: The Joy of the Gospel.* Washington, DC: United States Conference of Catholic Bishops, 2013.

Pramuk, Christopher. *At Play in Creation.* Collegeville, MN: Liturgical Press, 2015.

Prematilleke, L. "The Identity and Significance of the Standing Figure at the Gal-Vihar, Polonnaruwa, Ceylon." *Artibus Asia* 28, no. 1 (1966): 61–66.

Roche, Lisa, and Dan Turner, literary editors; Daniel A. Brown and Skip Schiel, photo editors. *Ashes and Light: Auschwitz to Hiroshima, Interfaith Pilgrimage for Peace and Life 1995.* Leverett, MA: Nipponzan Myohoji, 1996. http://teeksa photo.org/Archive/Exhibits/95PilgrF/AshesLightF/Ashes LightBook.html (accessed November 5, 2022).

Rohr, Richard. *The Divine Dance: The Trinity and Your Transformation.* London: SPCK, 2016.

Samy, Ama. "Interreligious Dialogue: Beyond Translation, Beyond Religion." *Dilatato Corde* 1, no. 2 (2011).

Sasaki, Rev. Chiemi Ishii. "Encounter with Takamori—Encounter with the Deep Stream." Her personal description with color photos of Chapel ("*Omidō*"), Memorial Wood, Koizumi Spring, fields, and symbols. Unpublished manuscript.

Sasaki, Rev. Chiemi Ishii. "The Idea/Image of Water That Runs Under the Ground—'Faith' for Shigeto Oshida." 2013 Sophia University Summer Theology Workshop. Translated by Chisato Kitagawa.

Scheuer, Jacques. *Enseignements de Vincent Oshida (1922–2003), un Maître Zen qui a rencontré le Christ.* Brussels: Voies de l'Orient, 2009.

Schiel, Skip. *Passing Through: Photographs on Pilgrimage; Auschwitz to Hiroshima, The Interfaith Pilgrimage for Peace and Life 1995.* http://teeksaphoto.org/Archive/Exhibits/95Pilgr.html (accessed November 5, 2022).

Schineller, Peter. *A Handbook on Inculturation.* Mahwah, NJ: Paulist Press, 1990.

von Schroeder, Ulrich. *Buddhist Sculptures of Sri Lanka.* Hong Kong: Visual Darma Public Ltd., 1992.

Steiner, George. "To Speak of Walter Benjamin." In *Benjamin Studies: Perception and Experience in Modernity.* Amsterdam: Rodopi, 2002.

Sutherland, Peter. "Walking Middle Passage History in Reverse: Interfaith Pilgrimage, Virtual Communitas and World-Recathesis." *Etnofoor* 20, no. 1 (2007): 31–66.

Verboven, Lucette. "Shigeto Oshida in gesprek met Lucette Verboven." (Interview with Lucette Verboven; in English with Dutch subtitles.) YouTube: https://www.youtube.com/watch?v=qwXMbGRKCT0&t=955s (accessed November 5, 2022).

Verboven, Lucette, ed. "Vincent Shigeto Oshida (Japan)." In *The Dominican Way*, 189–200. London: Continuum, 2011.